Procrastination Solutions for College Students

Procrastination Solutions For College Students

The Underground Playbook For Overcoming Procrastination
And Achieving Peak Performance

DENNIS STEMMLE

Procrastination Solutions For College Students

The Underground Playbook For Overcoming Procrastination And Achieving Peak Performance

© **2021 Dennis Stemmle**

ISBN-13: 978-1-7354030-1-4 (Paperback)

This book is
dedicated to:

Those students who will not let their lives be a shooting star that lights up the night sky for only a moment, but instead lives every day with real passion and purpose. For those students that choose to pursue the best version of themselves every day. For these students, better has no finish line! I admire your efforts, and I hope this book will provide encouragement and be a tool that will make your journey easier.

Praise For Procrastination Solutions For College Students

"Such an amazing book! This book has helped me to say no and focus on my own goals, along with much more. Definitely recommend this book." Julia Robinson, a student at Coastal Carolina University.

"WOW! After procrastinating most of my life, this book has helped me work on myself and my goals. The focus and productivity chapter was, by far, my favorite. A great read." Mickey McCullough-Cruz, a student at the University of Arizona.

"This book is great for anyone, especially college students, who are trying to progress in life and make better life choices. If you are looking for a self-help book, this is the one for you!" – John Gallardo, a student at the College of Charleston.

"It was great to read so many different experiences from people who I've never heard about before! It was great to know that I wasn't alone and that I can take back control of my life. Highly recommended!" Claudia Pisiack, a student at Arizona State University.

"As a student who wants to become a doctor, it was amazing to read the paragraphs on neurotransmitters and the brain! It was a fascinating read and something new to add to the argument of procrastination. This book is a 10/10!" – Julia Romano, a student at Texas State University.

"I was having pretty bad procrastination problems, especially with all my classes being online this semester. This book gave me the encouragement and the advice I needed to get back on track!" – Thomas Christaldi, a student at the University of Pennsylvania.

"I am a football player in college, and I absolutely loved this book! It showed me what it takes to not only excel on the field but in the classroom. "– Jarrett Guest, a student at Coastal Carolina University.

"I am in Terry College of business, and this book was a huge help for me. I read this book at a perfect time in my life!" – Zach Brooks, a student at the University of Georgia.

"This book spoke volumes for me and my teammates. I play football and go to school at one of the toughest institutions in America. I am very happy I was recommended this book." – Keyon Henry-Brooks, a student at Vanderbilt University.

"I am a senior in college and wish I would have read this book my freshman year! Nonetheless, I would highly recommend this useful book!" – Stephen Goodman, a student at the University of South Carolina.

"This was the perfect read for a business student. I can apply this to my daily life and even can help my peers!" – Mallory Lewis, a student at the University of Alabama.

"This book presents great insight into various student behaviors that are augmented by trifling excuses for not starting a task. Likewise, there are several remedies on how to increase the responsibility and accountability to the person you value most, yourself." – Ecaterina Soltoian, a student at RomaTre, Rome, Italy.

"Procrastination solutions for college students is a book that every child should read, not only college students. It offers great tips and strategies that are super beneficial and critical to learning as a young adult. These strategies have opened my eyes to what procrastination really is and how I can defeat it and no longer suffer from it." – James Marino, a student at Coastal Carolina University.

"Procrastination Solutions is a great book that provides terrific insight on how to manage the stress of being a college student. The 2-minute rule was especially helpful on how to deal with procrastination, and it's something that I've applied to my daily life. Professor Stemmle's book has helped me tremendously, and his ideas will be something that I apply to my life even after I graduate college." – Kelvin Arjuna, a student at Winthrop University.

"Procrastination Solutions For College Students allows a person to better understand how procrastination impacts life daily. This book provided me with insight into how to properly deal with procrastination and tips that can be applied to my life. This truly is an important read for any student to gain better knowledge on how to be successful in life." – Delilah Malczewski, a student at Tusculum University.

"This book shows how procrastination can affect daily routines and life. Learning the basic tendencies of wants and desires brings a new capability on how to work through the tough days that students go through. With these lessons, students will be able to focus and trained their minds to work past the struggle." – Tyler Stapleton, a student at the University of Tennessee.

"As a college student, I face problems every day when it comes to my workload. Procrastination is the biggest one. After reading this book, *'Procrastination Solutions for College Students,'* I have learned some new ways to overcome these everyday issues." – Owen Bratcher, a student at Coastal Carolina University.

"After reading this book, I realized that many of the reasons I procrastinate the way I do are due to my personal habits. Since reading this book, I have started changing these habits and have started doing better by completing work sooner." – Rachel Vick, a student at Clemson University.

"Procrastination is a leading cause for a student to not succeed in college, especially for students who have a big workload, like college normally offers. There are many ways to not procrastinate in college, and "*Procrastination Solutions For College Students*" clearly explains the best ways to overcome this terrible habit. This book is an asset for all college students, and I recommend it to all students that go to college." – Seth Skipper, a student at Clemson University.

"Like every other college student, I face day to day problems. We try and blame it on the teachers or even anyone other than ourselves. I know now I cannot blame anyone, but myself and I plan on using what I learned by reading this book to do a better job." – Kathleen Carl, a student at Horry Georgetown Technical College.

"Succeeding in college is the biggest goal I have set for myself so far in life. Procrastination is something that is trying to hold me back. As a student away from home, living a true college life, it is hard to stay on track. Especially since the COVID madness has started. There is so much time to do other things, and it causes me to procrastinate. After reading "*Procrastination Solutions for College Students,*" I now know what I need to do to fix my issue and succeed." Cameron Bailey, a student at The University of South Carolina.

"Procrastination has become a part of my study, which has been affecting the low quality of my study. This book shows me how to solve procrastination, and if you have the same problems as me, I recommend this book." – Charles Chen, a student at the University of South Australia.

"I found quite a few useful tips in this book that I plan to use for my remaining years of college!" – Jake Sarac, a student at P.I.A.

"Do you have procrastination? If you have one, you need *"Procrastination Solutions For College Students"* that will help you deal with your procrastination; It will help to improve your learning efficiency." – James Chen, a student at Coastal Carolina University.

"After reading this book, my pressure has been reduced a lot. It turns out that many college students have the same problems as me." – Phiraphat Wall, a student at Bangkok University.

"Procrastination is contagious. Treat it early and don't spread it to your friends." – Austin Parker, a student at Guangdong University of Foreign Studies.

"This book connected with me on a personal level and is filled with many tips to help one stop procrastinating." – Josh Mitchell, a student at Coastal Carolina University.

"I found this book interesting; it gave many useful tips regarding procrastination. Recommend to anyone who is a procrastinator!" – Ally DiMauro, a student at Coastal Carolina University.

"This book offers college students an opportunity to read about procrastination, enjoyed it very much!" – Mike LaRovera, a student at Salve Regina University.

"I wish I had this book earlier! Being home for classes this year has made me procrastinate 10x more. Having this book would have helped a million! Totally recommend." – Grace Simon, a student at Gateway Community College.

"I am currently studying nursing right now and have problems with procrastination. This book has helped me not procrastinate, and it has helped a lot. I have been motivated ever since." – Kaci Ricciuti, a student at Sacred Heart University.

"This book not only helps with school but with our everyday lives!" – Anna Marie Grice, a student at Clemson University.

"This book helps students who struggle with procrastination and can be helpful in these times more than ever." – Keishawn Brewton, a student at Buffalo University.

"I would recommend this book to every student in the world that wants to improve themselves that are not clear where to start." – Devi Cene, an International student from the University of Tirana.

"This is an amazing book that I would highly recommend college students read. Professor Stemmle really cares about his students and wants them to succeed!" – Dylan Huskins, a student at Coastal Carolina University.

"This is a must-read book if you need tips for succeeding in college WHICH ALL STUDENTS NEED!" – Blane Early, a student at Coastal Carolina University.

"I'm a student-athlete, and with everything, we have to do throughout the semester my teammates, and I do lots of our work last minute, with it being very relatable I thought this was a great book to read." – Cody Teodosio, a student at the University of New Haven.

"I took lots of tips from this book that I am going to try and use to procrastinate less. I would definitely recommend it to my friends!" – Luca Belenchia, a student at Central Connecticut University.

"Every college student needs to get their hands on this read. I'm going to defiantly take tips and work toward not procrastinating as I used to." – Sophie Kielmeyer, a student at the University of Delaware.

"Wow, I really enjoyed this read, great tips and very useful!" –Sage Borkowski, a student at Johnson and Wales University.

"For someone who is very guilty of procrastinating, this was a great read!" – Gianna DiLorenzo, a student at Coastal Carolina University.

"I have a major problem with procrastinating, but after reading this book, I have gained some helpful information on how to limit procrastinating!" – Holly Grice, a student at Coastal Carolina University.

"I found myself procrastinating more since everything has switched to online. This book is key to staying on track with my schoolwork." – Sophie Kirkley, a student at Horry Georgetown Technical College.

"After reading this book and being a freshman, it has helped me to realize staying ahead is easier than trying to catch up!" – Aly Poston, a student at Coastal Carolina University.

"This book is very important for young students and even adults because it teaches you how to build winning habits that will allow you to perform at a higher level." – B. Pressley, a student at the University of Virginia.

"I felt personally attacked by this book, but it was a good feeling because I learned about some bad habits I had and some ways to change them. I look forward to showing this book to my peers who might need it as I did." – Daven Cornelius, a student at Winston Salem State University.

"Great read, really considering making my students that I tutor read this book as a requirement." – Pamela Flowers, a student at East Carolina University.

"Procrastination Solutions for College Students is not only helpful but impressively informational! I highly recommend all college students read it!" – Jameah Moore, a student at Coastal Carolina University.

"Once you read the introduction, the rest of the book will be history! Must read!" – Jashayna Dobine, South Carolina State University.

"This book really explains the dangers of procrastination and offers college students advice on how to overcome it, which drives students to be more successful both academically and in their everyday lives." – Ava Carbone, a student at the University of California, Los Angeles.

"Balancing the life of a student-athlete and being a good student is an everyday battle, especially this year. This book is the instruction manual to an organized and efficient school experience!" – McKaellen Wilkerson, a student at Coastal Carolina University.

"This book provides a lot of statistics and real-world scenarios to help college students with advice on how to avoid procrastinating." – Sofia Sanchez, a student at Suffolk University.

"Procrastination solutions for college students is a great book. I would recommend it to any student who attends college" – James Williams, a student at West Chester University.

"Before reading this book, overcoming procrastination seemed impossible. Now, I understand why we procrastinate, and it has completely improved my productivity. This is an excellent read for college students!" – Travis Beni, a student at The College of New Jersey.

"Every college student is faced with procrastination challenges throughout their time in school. This is the perfect read to combat postponement of assignments." – Robert Parker, a Graduate student at Berkeley College.

"This book made my life so much easier, simply by using the solutions offered in this book. I highly recommend any college student read this book, especially if you're a procrastinator like me!" – Adam Godfrey, a student at Rider University.

"Procrastination is a big problem in college students. Sometimes I feel I am the only one who procrastinates. After reading this book, I don't feel alone at all and see that many students procrastinate. I never thought that procrastination was harmful to your body, but after reading this book, I understand why. I never thought there are as many changes to procrastinating as this book mentions." – Mya Maggorie, a student at East Stroudsburg University.

"This book opened up the gates of self-improvement for me. As a junior in college, procrastination has become a barrier to my success." – Amy Sheridan, a student at Montclair State University.

"Going to help a lot of high school seniors, this is a must-read." – Alyssa Kinney, a student at Sacred Heart University.

"Students may think they struggle alone, but it Is a lot more common than they may think, great book." – Audrey Larrow, a student at Quinnipiac University.

"Students who struggle with procrastinating definitely need to read this opened my eyes for sure" – Emilee Delfinis a student at Seton Hall University.

"Really enjoyed reading this, gave me some new insight into why I also might procrastinate on my assignments and how it affects me" – Kayley Byrne student at Southern Connecticut State University.

"I feel so identified with the section on the book that talks about controlling your brain. It means so much for me to control your emotions and your mind to focus on what is important and to keep improving in the fields you need to improve. This book overall covers a lot of the usual problems college students face day by day, it helps them feel identified with the topics and to use this knowledge to their own benefit." – Mauricio Pacheco, a student at Coastal Carolina University.

"I am HORRIBLE about waiting until the last second to do my work. This book could certainly teach me a thing or two about the benefits of NOT procrastinating." – Daniel Parham, a student at Hampden Sydney College.

"I wish I had bought this book before my freshman year; however, I think it could help me break some bad habits in procrastination." – Jase White, a student at Culver-Stockton College.

"I did not realize how much of a procrastinator I was until this book highlighted some of my habits. It's time to take into consideration some of these tips and skills!" – Charlotte Walker, a student at the University of North Carolina, Wilmington.

"Baseball sometimes becomes a priority over my grades. It's not laziness; it's schoolwork procrastination. This book is a lifesaver in my eyes." – Tyler White, a student at Lynn University Florida.

"This is definitely going to be my new BIBLE. Time to quit the procrastinating, I needed this book to call me out like it did!" – Sam Hodges, a student at Virginia Tech.

"I feel that I generally stay on top of my work, but this book will provide skills and tips to always improve." – Jake Smith, a student at Bridgewater College (Virginia).

"I really liked the idea behind the 'Two Minute Rule.' Both parts are really useful information." – Robbie Demarco, a student at James Madison University.

"The book makes excellent points about how making small changes can impact a lot in a person's life. This book is a great read!" – Jack Farello, a student at the College of Charleston.

"The book offers lots of great reasons and ways to change your mindset. I found them very insightful." – Liam Landree, a student at Rutgers University.

"I could've used this book for years now. It has tons of helpful information that a lot of college students could use." – Brian Forsman, a student at Brookdale Community College.

"This book is a great read for any college student who is looking for keys to success! I love this book." – Patrick Gilbride, a student at Coastal Carolina.

"This book is an awesome read for kids in college, and I'd recommend it to my fellow classmates and peers." – Cole Pearsall, a student at the College of Charleston.

"This book is the best gift I've received while I've been in college. It was an all-around great read." – Nick Izzo, a student at Coastal Carolina University.

"When reading this book, it was hard to put it down. I'll honestly probably read it again; it was such a good book." – Kevin Larco, a student at East Carolina University.

"As a college student, I tend to procrastinate on many of my assignments. Reading this book was very useful and gave me skills on how to be more productive instead of procrastinating: overall a great book!" – Paxton Masaracchia, a student at Coastal Carolina University.

"Keeping my focus can be difficult when doing homework. This book helped me learn how to stay focused and how focus increases productivity." – Owen Brenneman, a student at Lees Mcrae College.

"This book is amazing. I tend to always procrastinate. As a collegiate student-athlete who attends a military school, I always have a lot of work to do. This book has given me everything I need to improve on my time management to allow me to succeed in the following years. Would recommend to anyone." – Payden Masaracchia, a student at Norwich University.

"I think this book would be the key to getting my grades back on track." – Cole Finklestein, a student at the USC.

"This book was very helpful and insightful as a college student at a military school. I always struggle with procrastination and time management, and this has helped me greatly. I would recommend this book to anyone in the same position." – Nick Kandra, a student at Norwich University.

"Honestly, it is a struggle trying to figure out this college life as an athlete. We have many responsibilities because you must have your mind on the sport, but also keep up with academics and keeping up your grades. It is so hard to do both, but it is possible. I am slowly getting out of procrastination, but it is hard. Sometimes you do not want to think about work all the time. I am getting better, and with this book, I will put all of it into consideration. Thank you!" – Tim Ceaser, a student at Coastal Carolina University.

"While in high school, I did not struggle with procrastination because I guess I just did everything with ease. In college, it is a little different because there are more things to do in each class, and especially with the pandemic going on, it is hard to keep up. This does not mean it is impossible. I manage my time very well, and I get the hard stuff out the way and get the easy stuff later. A good idea is to write everything down, you must do each week on a sticky note and check it off each time you finish the assignment. It helps to organize each class assignment, and it is important to pace yourself." – Kendall Moore, a student at the University of Arkansas at Conway.

"I have always been one of those people who like to think that I don't procrastinate, but I often become victim to doing assignments late. This book is something I wish I would have read as a freshman because I can tell you from experience that all of the advice given is extremely accurate. Although I try to stay on top of things, I feel like this book gave me some new skills to work on in order to use my time more efficiently." – Jarrah Darboe, a student at Johnson C. Smith University.

"Actually, I struggle with procrastination when I did not know how college worked; the first year of college. It was a hard adjustment because I did not know what to expect, and I did not get why each class had assignments due at the same time, especially being an athlete. It can be hard because managing time to do the assignments and giving your all-in practice. It is important to pace yourself and to make time for your priorities. It is hard, but it is possible to do." – Josh Sanders, a student at Arkansas State University/Mid-South.

"This book is a great book for college students. Procrastination is a problem for lots of college students. This is a great read for students in general and definitely for students that are struggling with procrastination." – Keith Scott, a student at Coastal Carolina University.

"This book gives college students a guide of how to deal with procrastination, this book can help many students overcome their procrastination problem." – Tyra Wells, a student at Coastal Carolina University.

"This book offers a great way for students to handle college and how to handle their procrastination habits." – Keelin Scott, a student at Trident Technical College.

"This book can be a great guide for students to learn how to use their time wisely and to get rid of their study habits." – Kris Copeland, a student at Concord University.

"Although I may be one of the biggest procrastinators ever, this book really helped me see the true benefits of getting stuff done earlier. But I like that it actually explains the different ways to better handle things rather than just telling the reader to work ahead." – Jamar Darboe, a student at Coastal Carolina University.

"Procrastination is one of my biggest issues when it comes to school. This book is amazing, it has helped me so much. Definitely recommend!" – Joey Stanisic, a student at Harrisburg Area Community College.

"Although I may be one of the biggest procrastinators ever, this book really helped me see the true benefits of getting stuff done earlier. But I like that it actually explains the different ways to better handle things rather than just telling the reader to work ahead." – Jamar Darboe, a student at Coastal Carolina University.

"Definitely would recommend to others! Really connected with me." – Laura Markle, a student at the University of Connecticut.

Acknowledgments

When I first thought about writing this book, I wanted to be sure to acknowledge everybody who positively impacted my life and career. It is through others that I have gained my knowledge and experience that so powerfully contributed to me becoming the person I am today. I am eternally grateful for these mentors, coaches, and friends. This shared knowledge provided a foundation for any success that I have been fortunate enough to achieve in my life.

To all the college students that provided feedback and insights on this project, I am grateful for the time you took to make this book better.

To my son Bradley who strongly encouraged me to share my thoughts and ideas with college students everywhere.

To my wife, Karen, whose support has been endless.

Finally, a thank-you to the young men and women I have had the privilege to teach over the years. May you always choose to pursue the best version of yourself!

Table Of Contents

Introduction

"You may delay, but time will not, and lost time is never found again." — *Benjamin Franklin*

Procrastination Is A Goal Buster

Procrastination is a goal buster. Wait, it's more than that; it's a life buster. You might be thinking, isn't that a bit dramatic, Professor Stemmle? I have always procrastinated, and I have gotten along just fine! I am here to tell you, what got you here, won't get you where you want to go. You must raise your game! And if you only change one bad habit, make it to STOP procrastinating!

Shockingly, thirty percent of college freshmen drop out after their first year! And, only around half of the students who enroll in college end up graduating with a bachelor's degree. The average time-to-degree at the (so-called) four-year college hovers just over five years, with only one-third of students graduating in four years and another third taking six or more years to finish.

Behind these shocking facts and figures are millions of broken dreams, heartaches, and piles of mounting debt. You do not have to be one of those shocking statistics!

It's not their fault! Students and parents just don't realize the challenges faced in transitioning from high school to college. The skills students learned in high school don't transfer well to the unstructured college environment. In high school, the effects of procrastination are contained. Your parents, teachers, coaches, counselors, and advisors were on you non stop to ensure you got your work done. In college, that support system goes away, and your procrastination can easily get out of control.

We dedicate so much time, energy, and money to getting into college, but we give little thought to how to transition, how to be successful in this new environment. The simple reason why so many college students struggle is that they have not learned how to transition from the structured high school environment to the unstructured college environment. Procrastination, time management, and discipline are all skills that need to be greatly enhanced in college.

I never knew how big our education problem was until my son became one of those dreaded statistics mentioned earlier. As a top-performing high school student, he got into all his desired colleges, and we just never were worried about him performing well. However, his excitement from his college acceptances, the prospects of moving out of the house, and his embracing his independence, quickly led to frustration, stress, and surprise struggles.

After his first semester, our straight-A high school student found himself on academic probation. That's when I knew I had to figure out why millions of top high school seniors struggle to succeed in college.

I spent months talking to students, looking for similarities, trends, and kernels of knowledge that could help me understand the challenges and issues faced by students transiting from high school to college.

I gathered together all the tips, tricks, and suggestions from these students and transferred this knowledge to my son, who used this information to go from academic probation to Dean's List the very next semester (3.9 GPA). Only one B+ kept him off the President's List. As a result, I have made it my mission to help millions of high school seniors and underclassmen successfully transition to college and become more self-reliant, fulfilled, and successful.

Many folks wrongly believe procrastinators are lazy, stupid, or that they just do not care. But procrastination often emerges as a means of distancing oneself from stressful activities. People allocate more time to a task they judge as easy or fun than to tasks they judge as difficult or boring. By dealing with the underlying stressful aspects of the activities causing us to procrastinate in the first place, we can greatly reduce and contain our procrastination.

It's easy to put things off until later, especially when you dread the task. But in college, this is a real problem. If you put off your assignments or studying for tests, you are only hurting yourself. Procrastinating leads to stress and anxiety, not to mention poor performance. This starts a downward spiral that can be very difficult to recover from. With the help of this book, you CAN stop procrastination from busting your dreams and goals. I want you to achieve the success you deserve in life.

You Are Not Alone

Your procrastination struggles are much more common than you, your teachers, and your parents understand! Studies show that up to 95 percent of college students suffer from procrastination, approximately seventy-five percent of all students consider themselves to be procrastinators, and fifty percent of students procrastinate consistently and problematically.

The biggest challenge for procrastinators is just getting started. Most of the time, not starting seems to be related to a feeling of stress, fear, or simply a feeling of being overwhelmed with the whole process. Sometimes I hear students say they don't feel motivated to start their assignments; they are waiting for inspiration or a changing mood. I got news for you… people who wait on the mood to strike or motivation to suddenly hit them will find themselves doing everything last minute. Mood and motivation aren't prerequisites to action…it is a result of it! It doesn't matter how you feel. What matters is what you have to do to achieve your goals. You are an adult now, and a major part of being an adult is doing a bunch of crap you don't feel like doing!

What Is Procrastination, Anyway?

Procrastination is the action of delaying or postponing something to a later time. For example, you need to study for your mid-term exams but put off getting started until tomorrow, or the next day, or just maybe, the day after that. You find yourself scrolling social media, watching Netflix, or playing just one more game of Fortnite with friends. Many students don't even realize they are chronic procrastinators. Procrastination has become so ingrained in its approach that it has become a habit.

Students justify their behavior by telling themselves they perform at their best when they are under a tight deadline. Putting things off to do later has become a way of life. Other students procrastinate when they are afraid of doing something or when the task seems too difficult, scary, or they are simply bored with the task altogether. But those are just a few of the basic reasons why we procrastinate. In this book, we will dig deep into the topic of procrastination, why procrastination can keep you from performing your best, and how to overcome procrastination and become a world-class performer in your chosen field.

Procrastination Is A Nightmare For College Students

Procrastination will prevent you from performing at your best. It prevents you from getting the most out of your college experience. In short, procrastination will keep you from becoming the best version of yourself! Here are a few key reasons that procrastination is a problem for college students.

Good ideas take time. A recent study showed that the longer students waited to turn in an assignment, the worse their grades were, with last-minute hand-ins costing them five percentage points on average, or half a grade. Whether you are working on a small assignment or a large paper, good ideas take time to develop and come together in a well-thought-out cohesive fashion. Most written assignments in college will require you to select a topic, then spend time developing your thoughts around your ideas, revising your thoughts, and finally fine-tuning and polishing things up. If you procrastinate and wait until the last minute, you won't have time to properly go through an intellectual process required to ensure a fully reflective and developed piece of work. This also applies to things like essay questions on tests and exams. You need time to reflect on the question, rather than throwing out the first idea that pops into your head.

You will likely run out of time. Twenty-five percent of students report missing an assignment completely during the first two weeks of the semester. When it comes to strict deadlines-which is just about always in your college classes-you run the risk of missing the due date if you keep putting off your work until tomorrow. And the reality is that most professors will not give you an extension except in very special circumstances. It is not that they are trying to be mean, but once they make one exception, they will have to make hundreds. If your professor accepts late assignments, a grade penalty-often as much as one-third to one-half a grade a day will apply.

You might be being overly dramatic. One of the key reasons we all procrastinate is to avoid the pain associated with actually doing the task at hand. In my experience, students overestimate the pain they'll feel while completing their assignments. It's quite understandable when faced with a 15-page paper, a 25-question problem set, or 50 pages of reading, you naturally feel the task is enormous and overwhelming, and the simple thought of starting makes your stomach sick. The reality is, if you just get started on a small piece and then another small piece, then another manageable piece, etc., you will see the assignment coming together, and your fear will disappear as you build on the positive momentum you have created.

You lose your chance for help. Many students will want to enlist the help of a professor or a Teaching Assistant (TA). But their time is limited, and many professors only maintain office hours a few hours a week on specific days only, and not every TA is timely when it comes to getting back to students. With the majority of students waiting until the last minute, a classic supply vs. demand problem is created, especially if the assignment is challenging, and 75% of the students have figured out they are stuck three days before the assignment is due. By starting your assignments early, you won't lose the chance to consult with the professor or TA in case you have questions. Even if you get answers to your questions at the last minute, you will not have time to implement your professor or TA suggestions, which will destroy your grade. Your Professor or TA will hate taking their time and providing feedback and suggestions to see you completely ignore their advice.

Contrary to what you might believe. You won't work better under time constraints. If you put off your work until the last minute, your work will be hurried and will demonstrate the shortcuts you took due to the time pressure. This experience will likely create stress, anxiety, and even guilt for having put off the work once again. This behavior will take its toll on your sleep, energy, and mental well-being. It simply is not the best combination for your health or GPA.

Your work will look incomplete. One of the main differences between fair, good, and excellent work is that excellent work has gone through a natural cycle of thoughts, drafts, and revisions. The paper will flow naturally and follow a well thought out logical sequence. When the clock is ticking and your deadline is rapidly approaching, you will skip steps in the cycle and hand in an assignment that doesn't flow properly or hit on all the key ideas or concepts. Like a bad movie, the professor will easily notice the lack of effort that went into your work.

You place yourself at a relative disadvantage. While you're busy being busy, putting off your work for another time, some of your fellow students are getting down to business and getting started on their assignments. These students are likely going to raise the bar for everyone and increase the gap between excellent work, good work, and average work. Many professors will fit their grade curves to a somewhat normal distribution or even limit the percentage of students receiving an "A." Most universities expect the grades in a class section to follow a somewhat normal distribution or average grade target, ensuring a class is neither too difficult nor too easy. The university won't talk about this in their orientations or course program guides, but rest assured behind those pillars of knowledge and opportunity, proper course curve fitting is being discussed and expected.

The task is probably not as hard as you think. The reality is that thousands of students just like you have completed the task at hand. It's often hard to determine at the start of an assignment just how much time it'll take you to complete the assignment-especially if the topic is unfamiliar or covers a diverse area of topics. Just get started, and you will likely find that things are not as bad as you have built them up to be.

The task is the task. Some students think that somehow the task is going to get easier if they wait a little longer. If they give it a little more time, some miracle or inspiration will strike that will change the course of the assignment forever. Of course, this isn't going to happen; the assignment is the assignment once your professor assigned it. Get over it, and in the words of Nike, Just Do It!

Life happens. Anytime you have an assignment that covers some extended length of time or involves some research, or builds upon prior lessons, there is an increased likelihood that something distracting and unexpected will arise. This unexpected event leads to stopping or greatly slowing down your ability to complete your work. You could catch the bug spreading around campus at the speed of a viral YouTube video. You could get food poisoning from the campus cafeteria. Another professor could spring an assignment on you that requires unscheduled time. Some work or family emergency could pop up. Whatever the event, you can count on life getting in the way, and if you have properly planned and allowed some room in your schedule for these unplanned events, you will be able to deal with things and not tank your GPA.

Balancing class loads, assignments, work, and of course, fun can lead to a great deal of stress for the average college student. It's important to realize that this feeling is normal, and you are going to feel stressed with so much going on in your life. You can easily start to feel like your life is spiraling out of control, but you're not alone, and your fellow students are feeling somewhat the same way. Consider the following:

- 85% of college students reported they had felt overwhelmed by everything they had to do at some point in the past year.

- 42% of college students stated anxiety as a top concern.

- 30% of college students reported that stress had negatively affected their academic performance.

Chapter 1:
Why People Procrastinate &
How It Is Harmful

"Procrastination is the bad habit of putting off
until the day after tomorrow what should have
been done the day before yesterday."
Napoleon Hill

I told myself I'd begin writing first thing this morning and crank out a few pages of a paper due tomorrow. It's 1:55 P.M., and I am just now sitting down to write. Why did I procrastinate on this? Sound familiar? You know your not the only one to procrastinate. We've all done it. We refer to ourselves as the king or queen of procrastination in a totally self-defeating way.

Instead of doing the task needed, we find ourselves putting it off. Maybe you have a report due. But instead of doing it, you find yourself watching Netflix, cruising the internet, chatting on social media, doing the laundry, or a million other things. People have suffered from procrastination since early times, as seen in the classic Greek poet Hesiod. He wrote in his poem:

Works and Days
Do not postpone for tomorrow
or the day after tomorrow;
barns are not filled by those who postpone
and waste time in aimlessness.
Work prospers with care;
He who postpones wrestles with ruin.

Someone who postpones and wastes time in aimlessness could be the description of today's procrastinator. It's easy to procrastinate. We can simply put off the task until later. In fact, a recent study showed that some 95 percent of college students procrastinated on a regular basis, most often when it came to completing assignments and coursework. Procrastination, it seems, has become part of our DNA.

Why Do People Procrastinate?

When you think of someone who procrastinates, you probably think they are lazy and unmotivated. This is the commonly held view of what procrastination is. It's the belief that procrastinators don't know how to manage their time. While procrastination and time management are two core challenges for college students, they are typically two separate issues.

Although some of the time, it might be connected, this is not always the case. New research into the psychology of procrastination suggests the problem is not only with your willpower but with your emotions and other factors. In fact, procrastination is a result of psychological, inherited, and environmental factors.

If you are interested in diving deeper into the area of time management, pick up a copy of my bestselling book, "*Time Management Secrets For College Students.*" Let us examine the reasons why we procrastinate more closely.

Psychological or Emotional?

"Procrastination is not a time-management problem, it's an emotion-management problem," says Tim Pychyl, an associate professor of psychology at Carleton University and contributor at *Psychology Today*.

Our mood and emotions regulate how we feel when approaching an activity. Procrastination is then an emotion management issue. Positive emotions have us jumping into the activity. For example, if we expect a task or activity to feel good, we go for it, like tailgating, playing video games, or eating ice cream.

Negative emotion, on the other hand, means we will do what we can to avoid feeling bad. For example, we feel resistance towards doing our taxes, writing research papers, going to that statistics class, or doing school or work tasks.

Things that cause us to feel bored, uncomfortable, afraid, frustrated, etc., causes us to procrastinate. Instead of forcing ourselves to do the task, we procrastinate by doing things that give us a good feeling. Our emotions cause us to procrastinate.

"Medical imaging studies have shown that mathphobes, for example, appear to avoid math because even just thinking about it seems to hurt," explains Barbara Oakley in *A Mind for Numbers*. "The pain centers of their brains light up when they contemplate working on math."

It's always the same thing. We want to do what we need to do even if it feels bad and brings up some resistance. We have intentions of following through, but our negative emotions make us feel uncomfortable. We then avoid the task for as long as possible by doing something that is more enjoyable.

Our Genes

Some researchers think procrastination is an inherited trait. Researchers from the University of Colorado did a study of human twins. They found that identical twins share more similarities in their behavior as compared to fraternal twins. The study showed that procrastination, just like impulsivity, is inherited. They believe this trait comes from our nomadic ancestors as a foundation for survival.

Environmental Influences

Often there are things in our daily lives that we perceive as a cause for our procrastination. These excuses of why we procrastinate often include family obligations taking up our time and people or situations that cause us to procrastinate. We blame our circumstances when we put off doing something. Sometimes we blame procrastination on not having the right tools or that we cannot work any faster (meaning we need to be more productive). But you cannot blame procrastination on one thing and magically be able to change it. In fact, both conscious and subconscious traits are the reason that we procrastinate.

Reasons We Procrastinate

One of the things we do when we procrastinate is to use excuses. These excuses are often founded in our subconscious as fears, anxiety, or some other form of behavior that keeps us from acting.

- **Fears or anxieties**. Fear of failure is one of the top reasons students procrastinate. We fear the unknown and procrastinate to avoid pain. Fear of failure includes a low self-confidence level, anxiety over what will happen if you fail, and fear you cannot meet your own expectations.

- **Avoidance**. We do everything we can to avoid an unpleasant situation. We procrastinate to avoid being told no or ridiculed. We stay in our comfort zone to avoid rejection.

- **Overwhelm**. Procrastinators often avoid tasks because they do not know where to begin. They don't break the big project down into little projects but try to tackle it all at once. Or they have several small tasks that all need to be done, and they do not know where or which one to begin with. So instead of doing the tasks, they avoid doing any of them as long as they can.

- **Overconfidence**. Some procrastinators are so confident in the task that they need to do that they put it off to the last minute. They believe they know how to do the task or are confident they can complete it without preparation, so they put it off.

- **Perfectionism**. Along the same lines as overconfidence, perfectionism keeps you from doing or finishing a task. Perfectionism is often described as someone who pays excessive attention to detail, resulting in the preoccupation with a task that causes them to not complete the tasks. They procrastinate for fear that they won't do the job right.

- **Lack of motivation and accountability**. Sometimes, we don't have an immediate deadline, but we might have all semester to work on a paper or project.   These long timelines keep students from starting as they think they have lots and lots of time. Procrastinators may set goals but lack the motivation or someone to hold them accountable to reach them.

- **Indecisiveness**. Students procrastinate because they can't make decisions quickly. They can't decide which course of action to take or which decision to choose before they can move forward with action. Over-thinking the situation leads to analysis paralysis.

- **Vague or abstract goals**. When your goals are vague, you are more likely to procrastinate than if you had clearly defined goals. A vague goal like "start exercising" is more likely to lead to procrastinating than a more concrete one like "go to the gym every day after class or walking on the treadmill at high speed for 30 minutes."

- **Disliking the task**. Procrastination often happens when you are averse to the task you need to do. When you find a task unappealing, you're more likely to want to do anything to avoid it. There are many things about a task that might cause you to procrastinate. The task might be frustrating, boring, or tedious. You might procrastinate because of your lack of competence in doing the task.

- **Attention Deficit Hyperactivity Disorder (ADHD).** Procrastinators often blame their ADHD. They say their disorder makes it hard for them to concentrate on a single task for long; instead, they jump from task to task without finishing any. Although research shows that there is a significant correlation between ADHD and procrastination, the symptom of inattention is the main reason for procrastination by those who have ADHD.

- **Depression**. Someone suffering from depression will often procrastinate. This is because depression causes them to have difficulty concentrating, have fatigue, and a reduced interest in most activities.

- **Low energy levels**. This can be either physical energy or mental energy. Tired after a full day of classes can make you procrastinate towards things you need to take care of.

- **Laziness**. Your intrinsic unwillingness to put forth the effort to do what you need to is a driving force behind procrastination. Laziness, however, is often caused by an underlying reason, such as anxiety or fear of failure.

While these are not all the reasons we procrastinate, these are certainly the most common forms of procrastination that face students.

Why Procrastination Is Harmful

"There is nothing so fatal to character as half-finished tasks." — *David Lloyd George*

No doubt, you are starting to understand why you have been procrastinating, but did you know that continued procrastination can be harmful to you in many areas of your life?

People who are chronic procrastinators find they pay their bills late, start work on big projects the night before they're due, do their holiday shopping the day before the holiday, or file their income tax returns after the deadline. Procrastination can lead to pain and frustration in many areas of your life.

Your Health

Procrastination can affect how students see themselves, their stress levels, and even their health. Stress itself can have negative impacts on your health, including insomnia, headaches, colds and flu, high blood pressure, stiff muscles, and obesity.

Chronic procrastinators also can delay healthy behaviors like eating right, exercising, or getting enough sleep. Students put themselves in a position where they have to pull all-nighters, so they don't sleep, they are forced to pump their body full of sugar and caffeine for needed energy, and of course, this leads to the body eventually crashing. When compounded over time, this behavior can lead to diabetes or heart disease, as well as low energy levels, depression, anxiety, and even a shorter life span.

Procrastinators often have a lack of self-control. This can lead to engaging in activities that might physically cause harm, such as smoking, alcohol and drug abuse, and overeating. Risky behaviors may also be a factor in poor choices like unprotected sex and driving recklessly.

Your Social Life

Procrastination can also harm your social life as well. When you put things off, you are putting a burden on others to pick up the slack. Your family, friends, group members, or others who depend on you can become resentful when you wait until the last minute to do something. Maybe you end up having to cancel dates, leave a party early, or let your sorority sisters or fraternity brothers down.

I see many students flip the script entirely, leaning into their social life so hard to make up for the lost time that they find themselves letting others down and end up on academic probation. Overcome procrastination, manage your time effectively, and you will have plenty of time for all the social activities you desire.

Your Success

"My mother always told me I wouldn't amount to anything because I procrastinate. I said, just wait." — Judy Tenuta

Procrastinators are underachievers. They normally operate under their full potential. They are wasting time watching Netflix, gaming, surfing social media, or the internet, or any other form of distraction instead of working hard and getting things done.

Procrastinators struggle to plan and have a hard time understanding the long-term impact of their immediate decisions. And when they do, they struggle to follow through and often fall short of their best work in the end because they procrastinated and made excuses why they could not get started.

When you procrastinate, you take the risk of a bad grade, missing an assignment altogether, or missing out on scholarships, internships, and professor recommendations. You are looked over because of your lack of consistency in your performance. Being a chronic procrastinator can damage your reputation as well. If you miss deadlines or say you will do something but don't, it is simply making empty promises to others and yourself. People will see this and stop depending on you.

Every semester I have students email me about a missed assignment during the first few weeks of class. They tell me how seriously they take their work and how this is just not like them. I can tell you from experience, on nine out of ten occasions, it is exactly like them. Procrastination is so engrained in their behavior that they honestly tell themselves a narrative that is completely disconnected from reality.

As I write this, I had a student just two days ago email me that she had missed an assignment for a second time. She was not sure how it happened and explained how she was taking three summer courses and how difficult it was to keep up. Her first email told me how seriously she took her work and how missing an assignment was just not like her. I looked her up and saw she was repeating the class, had never been on the Dean's List, and was trying to knock out some required classes during the summer so she could graduate on time. Was she telling me a story? Telling herself a story? My guess is a little of both. Procrastinators have the best intentions, but they often fail to understand that their inaction has consequences.

Your Life Satisfaction

"The really happy people are those who have broken the chains of procrastination, those who find satisfaction in doing the job at hand. They're full of eagerness, zest, and productivity. You can be, too."—Norman Vincent Peale

Procrastinators are not as happy as those who are successful and productive. They are unhappy because they are less successful in their studies, career, relationships, finances, health, and any number of other areas of their life.

People who procrastinate tend to be very self-critical. They put off doing what they would like to do or need to do and then give

43

themselves a mental beating over it. This type of self-sabotage results in even more procrastination.

Having a life filled with constant disappointment and self-criticism keeps them from finding happiness. They feel guilty for not doing what needs to be done, for letting others down, and for their own lack of follow-through.

Procrastinators often start to feel like their life is one of missed opportunities, wasted potential. They feel shame, guilt, and disappointment. This can lead to low self-esteem that creates even more unhappiness and frustration.

Next Steps

So far, you have learned why we procrastinate and how it affects you and those around you. You learned that procrastination can be a real problem in your life if left unchecked. Procrastination, however, doesn't necessarily have to be a serious problem for you. All of us procrastinate from time to time, and unless procrastination begins to have a serious impact on your daily life and health, procrastination can be seen as a simple challenge, a behavior that you need to make.

We procrastinate because we don't want to do something because it's boring, or we don't know how to do it, or we just don't see why it is even necessary to start with. Procrastinators are known for their excuses. They have one for almost every situation. For example, if they have a big project due soon, they might use the excuse that they don't know where to start or, on the opposite end of the spectrum, that the project is easy for them, so they can wait until the last minute to tackle it.

Begin by looking at the real reason you procrastinate. Next time you catch yourself saying you'll do it later, stop and really examine why you are putting it off.

- Are you afraid you will fail because you always have in the past?
- Is procrastination something you saw growing up in your family?
- Have you allowed procrastinating to become a habit because you are lazy or just not interested in the task?
- Maybe it's due to your self-esteem level, confidence in your abilities, or your negative thoughts that keep you from taking action.
- Maybe you are a perfectionist. You are thinking everything has to be perfect before you can start or finish a task.   This way of thinking can keep you stuck and constantly putting off a task until you believe you can do it perfectly.

Now that you know why you procrastinate, you can begin taking steps to start changing that behavior. I will give you a few ideas that will get you started.

The "5-Second Rule."

Mel Robbins wrote the book, *The 5-Second Rule*, and while you may not be familiar with her work, this rule is not about eating food dropped on the floor if you can pick it up in less than 5-seconds.

The "5-second rule" focuses on the neuroscientific foundations for how our minds work when we procrastinate. The idea behind this rule is that it requires you to disarm and decapitate procrastination by taking necessary action within the first five seconds because the longer you put off action, the higher your risks of procrastinating.

Our brains are naturally wired toward our own self-preservation. So, whenever we experience stress, such as when we must wake up in the morning or having to exercise when we don't feel like it, our brains take those signals that something is wrong. This puts the subconscious mind into the fight or flight mode to try to preserve the body through inaction in an attempt to pre-empt dangers from happening. It results in feeling more and more sluggish, causing us to procrastinate.

However, with the "five-second rule," you don't give the subconscious mind the time to build momentum and yield its power. By acting against its wishes to procrastinate, you nip the procrastination problem in the bud. When you act within the first five seconds, you set your body in motion, which in turn creates emotion. So, by getting up and immediately moving, you will be able to create a counter-emotion that makes you want to continue moving forward.

So, when you feel the temptation to put off working on the first few tasks of the day, just count backward from five. As you get closer to zero, act. Action will break the inertia, and motion will create emotion. The more you can do this on a consistent basis, the quicker you can develop a habit that will stop procrastination for good.

If a task is too long to complete in the time you have available, then use the five seconds to schedule the task or activity for a time you can complete the task. To-Do Lists only work if the items on the list get scheduled. Otherwise, your list will just continue to grow and will become unmanageable, and then you just procrastinate more.

The "2-Minute Rule."

The "2-Minute Rule" builds on the "5-second rule," and it is a real lifesaver. It helps you overcome procrastination and laziness by making it very easy to get started. The hardest part of almost any task is just getting started! There are two parts to the "2-Minute Rule."

Part One — If it takes less than two minutes, then do it now.

Part I comes from David Allen's bestselling book, *Getting Things Done*. It is amazing just how many small tasks that we put off that we could get done in two minutes or less. For example, texting your mom or dad, tossing the laundry in the washing machine, sending that email to your group, checking your university email, reviewing your calendar for any assignments, and so on. If a task takes less than two minutes to complete, then do it right now.

Part Two — When you start a new habit, it should take less than two minutes to do.

"Once we begin a task, no matter how dreaded, our perceptions of the task change...we don't appraise the task as quite so stressful or difficult once we get started. Starting is everything."— Tim Pychyl

Can all of your tasks, assignments, and goals be accomplished in two minutes? Of course not! But that really is not the point. The point is everything can be started in two minutes. And that's the power behind this rule. It works for one simple reason: the reality of real life. I heard a speaker at Google talk about meditation. He said most people say they don't have twenty minutes to meditate. He said he tells them to meditate for two minutes, or one minute, even 30 seconds. He has found that once people got started, often, they kept going.

When I told students, who were overcome with stress and anxiety about writing a paper for half a day, I told them to just write for two minutes. They were like, I can do that! You see, they had built up the task to be so much work in their mind; the pain to start was just too great. Later, in this book, I will discuss the Pomodoro technique. The Pomodoro technique will not just get you started but will provide you with a system to help elevate your productivity to new levels. But for now, just start. If you get on a roll, keep going, it really is that simple. Remember that proverb, "A journey of a thousand miles begins with a single step."

Every time you catch yourself falling into the old procrastination pattern, stop and ask yourself, is this behavior helping you or keeping you from reaching your goals. Then, just start the task.

Chapter 2:
Procrastination and
Your Goals

"A year from now, you may wish you had started today." — ***Karen Lamb***

In chapter one, we covered the basics of procrastination, and I even gave you a couple of quick rules to get you started in your journey to overcoming your procrastination. After all, I don't want you procrastinating on getting started until the end of this book!

But can procrastination really be that bad? After all, it has worked just fine for you to this point. Well, it turns out there are two types of procrastination. The first type is procrastination occurs on things with deadlines. In these situations, the damage of procrastination is contained by the deadline itself. In college, your work has deadlines. With these deadlines in hand, you procrastinate, but eventually, that looming deadline creates enough stress and anxiety that you get started and complete your task. Sure, you tell yourself you will never do this again, you will manage your time better, but the cycle just seems to repeat itself.

The damage in these situations is typically contained to a lower grade, higher stress, and anxiety, but most students work their way through it, and by the end of the first semester of their second year, they have developed a system that works for them. It is not ideal, it doesn't allow them to perform at their best, but it works.

The problem is that one-third of students never make it to that point; they find themselves overwhelmed, they think college isn't for them, they think they are not smart enough, or their poor performance led to lost scholarship money and or parental support, and they were forced drop out.

Another 20% of students make it past that third semester but never figure it out and don't end up graduating. In the end, half of the students who attend college never graduate. In my experience, the vast majority of those students fail because of bad habits, lack of discipline, procrastination, and poor time management skills. The students academic work was not the issue; self-management was the real issue.

While deadlines help many students overcome their procrastination, it does not ensure that students do their best work, are prepared, or even understand what they were actually working on.

The really bad kind of procrastination, the type of procrastination that can derail your life, is when you procrastinate on things that have no deadlines, nothing to force you to take action. Maybe you wanted to go to graduate school after a couple of years of work, but life got in the way. Two years turned into three, and three turned into five, and now ten years later, you are married with a kid or two, and that dream seems like a distant wish.

Maybe you wanted to start a business someday, but with no deadline and a good-paying job, that someday turns into never. The real problem is that your hopes, your dreams, these things rarely come with deadlines, so you never get started. You wake up one day and wonder what happened? How did you get here? You feel empty and sad as you wanted so much more out of life. Procrastination robbed you of your dreams!

This is why it is so important to write down your goals and dreams and make a plan complete with resources needed and, of course, a clear deadline. Written goals can serve to mitigate the damage of procrastination and help keep your life on track.

"If you want to be happy, set a goal that commands your thoughts, liberates your energy and inspires your hopes." — *Andrew Carnegie*

Goal Setting Made Simple

To get what you want from life, you first need to know what it is you want. After all, how can you fulfill your potential if you do not know where you want to go, who you are, or what makes you happy? Now, most of you are probably thinking I have no idea what I want to do with my life yet! This is more than ok and quite expected. Figuring out life's big questions takes time, and goal setting is such a crucial step in that journey.

Learning how to effectively use goals to get the most out of your life is a critical skill set to obtain. If you do not know what your goals are, then life becomes a little like going on a journey with no destination in mind. Even though you might enjoy the journey, you are still going to risk ending up somewhere you don't want to be, and you certainly won't take the most efficient route to get there!

Sounds simple, right? You have to ask yourself what you really want from life and then go and get it. Right? Unfortunately, it's not. Regrettably, goal setting is anything but easy and is very much a skill in itself. The problem is that not many people realize this, and they never think to assess the quality of the goals themselves. They blame their motivation, their circumstances, or even other people. But rarely do they assess whether the issue might be with their goals themselves.

What are your goals? Really, what are your goals? Do you want to make the Dean's List, discover your passion, land a job, skate by with any degree? Goals are important for everyone, and identifying them upfront helps you stay focused along the way.

Why set goals? Life is very unstructured and has a way of getting away from you. At any given moment, there are thousands of possibilities, new bright shiny objects, a new viral cat video, a few hundred social media posts from friends, and a host of other things you could do.

When you prepared to get your driver's license, you took driver's education; you practiced hours on end, you learned the rules of the road. When you went for your driver's test, the tester told you where to go, where to turn left, turn right, speed up, turn around, etc. You just did not hop in the car and decide to drive to Alaska to see some Kodiak bears and demonstrate your great driving skills along the way. But what is it that keeps you from ending up in Alaska? The answer is that you got into your car with a clear goal of getting that driver's license you had dreamed about for years! You knew at the beginning exactly what your goal was, and you had a clear plan, and you stayed focused on that plan.

Life is the same way. If you know at the beginning where you want to go, you will probably get there. Even if detours and delays arise, eventually, you will get there. But if you do not know where you're going, you probably won't end up at a point that makes you happy.

But what if I don't know where I want to go? That's ok. At most universities, your first two years are filled with a common core, your Math, English, Sciences, etc., set a goal for yourself to perform well in those classes. Work a few courses into your schedule that you think you might enjoy. Set a goal to pick a major after you have had time to explore some different opportunities. This approach will allow you to divide your goals into time frames (immediate goals, short-mid-term goals, and long-range goals). You don't have to have firm answers to those gripping questions about what you want to be or do when you're done at college to make this work; your goals are likely to shift and change over time anyway. All you need to do right now is think of a handful of goals to get started. Write down a list of goals now before reading further.

An Example of Bad Goal Setting

To understand how to write a good goal, it can help first to take a look at what makes a bad goal. Why is it that some goals don't work out the way they should? What should we do differently to avoid this happening the next time?

Let's imagine for a moment that you want to get into shape. You're planning on losing weight and building muscle – which is a pretty common goal that an awful lot of students are interested in accomplishing.

In this example, a typical goal might involve writing down the ideal body weight and measurements that you are trying to reach and then setting yourself a target – three months, six months, or one year. And then you get to it! But this is a goal that is destined to fail. Why? Because this goal is far too vague, far too distant, and far too out of your control.

Let us fast forward two weeks, at which point you have hopefully been training hard for a while and changing your diet. Suddenly, life starts to get in the way. You find yourself bogged down with other things you must do, like preparing for that upcoming exam, paper, or party on Friday night, and you don't have the time or the energy to make it to the gym today. Or tomorrow. And the day after that is looking shaky as well.

But you tell yourself it is okay because you don't need to work out. Not working out on those days is not breaking your goal. You have plenty of time to reach your goal, and it is up to you how you are going to go about making it happen. So, if you take time off today, you will just put some more time in tomorrow. Or the next day. If this week is a write-off, then you can always make up for it next week. And so, it continues, week after week, until you get to the end of your allotted time span, and you have blown any chance of accomplishing that goal.

Or how about this alternative scenario? Imagine that you did put in the time, and you worked very hard every day to get into shape. But the pounds just did not come off. Maybe this is due to a slow metabolism. Maybe it boils down to those late-night snacks or just too much partying. Either way, you get to a certain point, and you realize once again that you are not going to make it even though you tried your best. So, what do you do? You give up, disheartened, and you quit trying.

A Better Goal

Now let's imagine that same scenario, but this time we approach our goal differently. What would a good goal look like if you wanted to lose weight or build muscle?

For starters, you should remove the time element. Instead of aiming to accomplish something in X number of days, how about you instead aim to do something toward your goal every day. Look at the goal that you want to accomplish, and then break that down into much smaller steps. To lose weight, let's say you need to eat 1,800 calories or less a day. And you need to work out three times a week for an hour each day. If you can stick to this plan, then you will eventually notice changes – be they big or small.

Instead of focusing on the end goal, set yourself a daily plan. A daily goal is something that is entirely within your control – meaning that you cannot "fail" for reasons outside of your control. It is also completely resistant to being put off or delayed. You can't "work out today" tomorrow! Likewise, a slow metabolism is not going to prevent you from eating only 1,800 calories.

I learned this concept from actor/comedian Jerry Seinfeld. Jerry developed a technique that he uses to make sure he sticks to these kinds of goals, and he calls it "The Chain." The idea is that he builds a chain each day as he completes his daily goal, each day represents a new link in his chain, and this process creates immense pressure not to break the chain. For Jerry, the process of writing one new joke each day allowed him to craft his skills and provided the foundation for his tremendous long-term success.

An easy way to implement this strategy is with a calendar and a pen. Every day that you successfully achieve 1,800 calories or less, you put a tick on the calendar for that day. Your daily tick marks will start to build up gradually, and over time, you will come to feel proud of that row of ticks and not want to ruin it by missing one. You will not want to "break the chain."

Whether you use this approach or not, the point is that you should write goals that are immediate and simple. Meanwhile, you can let the overarching objective "take care of itself."

Is Your Goal Too Ambitious?

There is nothing wrong with an ambitious goal. Many people say that "dreaming big" can even make you more likely to accomplish your aim because it attracts attention, gravitates people toward you, and helps get people on board. If you tell people you want to fly to space, you will get a lot more positive attention than if you tell people you want to climb Stone Mountain (a quartz monzonite dome formation just outside Atlanta, Georgia).

Therefore, another piece of advice that often gets thrown around is for you to "have visions, not goals." Visions are abstract, and they are grand. These are things you visualize and dream about, rather than things you write down and tick off. If you want to get into shape, then your goal can be to train three times a week, but your vision would be to become the best physical specimen you can – attractive to everyone and full of confidence and energy.

But while a vision can be as grand and extreme as you like, those smaller steps should still be small, and they should be easy. At least at the very start, your plan should be easy, and this will then allow you to build towards your higher overarching objective. Think of this as a pyramid. At the top, you have your grand vision for the future – something so exciting that it helps you to launch yourself out of bed in the morning. Beneath that, you might have your 'realistic' version of what you can achieve with your current resources. Beneath that, you might have the steps you are taking every day to achieve it.

The mistake a lot of people make is to lump all these things together and not to consider the necessary sequencing required to move from one level to the next. Lumping is the reason that someone who has never been to the gym before might well write themselves a new training program that requires them to train for an hour a day, seven days a week, and to do this on a diet of 1,000 calories. Is it any wonder that they don't tend to stick to their plan and fail to reach their goals?

Impatience is your enemy when it comes to writing good goals. People want to accomplish their goals now. They don't want to put in the time or the repetitious work that it takes to reach their goals. And they certainly don't want the fear that comes from the uncertainty that after all their work, they might not achieve their goals.

But you need to change that thinking. Everything worth having comes with work and diligence, and this is often highly repetitive and boring. If you want to get into shape, you need to train regularly, and it takes years to get to a point where your new physique is impressive and permanent. If you want to start your own business after college, well, then there is a ton you need to learn before you even get going. Procrastinating on a goal is just as bad, by the way – which is another reason it is so important you have a clear plan of action!

A good way to understand this process is to look at the world of video gaming. Video games begin with a few levels that are incredibly easy to prevent you as the player from getting discouraged quickly and quitting. Craft your goals the same way – if your "level one" is a massive, difficult battle, then you will not be successful.

Let's look at running. Lots of people get it wrong when they are taking up running for the first time. Here, they aim to start running long distances right away and losing weight. It's grueling, painful, and unrewarding, and it leaves them gasping and achy for days after.

What they should do is to first focus on getting good at running and on learning to like running. That means running short distances, not running too fast, not running too far, and generally not pushing themselves beyond a sensible point. This way, they can gradually start to like running, and they can gradually find themselves running further and further without even trying.

Often, it only takes small changes to get to the place you want to be. The Japanese notion of "Kaizen" best exemplifies the impact of small changes. Kaizen essentially means lots of small changes that build up to significant results.

For instance, if you want to graduate with a 3.7 or higher GPA, then it might be easier to look at small changes you can make to get there rather than massive ones.

- Go to class every day.
- Create note cards after each lecture.

- Make sure you get 7 hours of sleep every night.

- Commit to the use of your daily planner.

- Visit your professors during their office hours.

These are just a few small changes that should be easy enough for most students to stick to, and yet they can be enough to impact your GPA total in your favor – eventually leading to a cumulative GPA of 3.7 or better!

Look at your current goals. How many of the tasks that you intend to complete today contribute to accomplishing the goals you have set for yourself? Are you actively working on these goals? Are you procrastinating, putting key tasks off for a later time? What would you have to change about your life to make your goals a priority? What activities are taking you away from your goals? How can you eliminate or reduce these distractions?

Breaking your goals into manageable pieces can help. Once you have a set of goals, it is useful to decompose the goals into manageable steps or sub-goals. Decomposing your goals makes it possible to tackle them one small step at a time and to reduce any tendencies to procrastinate.

Consider, for instance, the goal of obtaining your college degree. This goal can be broken down into four sub-goals. Each sub-goal is the successful completion of one year of your program. These sub-goals can be further broken down into individual courses within each year. The courses can be broken down into tests, exams, term papers, etc., within the passage of the sixteen weeks of classes each semester. Each week is broken down into individual days, and each day into hours and minutes you'll spend in your classes and doing homework for each day.

While it may seem a bit overwhelming to think about all the activities that will go into earning that college degree, thinking of your goals in smaller chunks helps to reinforce the idea that there is a connected path linking what actions you take today and the successful completion and earning of your degree. Seeing these connections can help you monitor your progress and detect whether you are on track or not. Take some time now to think through the goals you've set and to break them down into their smaller constituent parts.

Pro Tip – Many students struggle with setting goals, and that is quite normal, you have your whole life ahead of you, and your goals will change. The idea here is to select goals that will give you the most options, open the most doors for you in the future. For instance, if all else is equal, a Marketing degree will give you more options than a degree in Ancient Animal Bite Marks. When in doubt, when uncertain, choose the path that gives you the most future options.

Now that you have made a list of goals, I want you to re-experience them in your mind by visualizing the steps you will take to achieve your goals. Visualizing the steps you will act on to obtain your goals increases the probability of achieving your goals. Successful athletes pre-experience over and over in their minds how they are going to perform in a game, so they can be at their peak effectiveness once game day arrives. You can take the pre-experience from athletes and directly apply the method to any goal you want to achieve.

One mistake many students make in seeking a goal is that they can focus so much on reaching the goal, the end state reward, that they fail to enjoy their college experience. Many students are in such a hurry to graduate and start their careers that they do not get the most out of this time in their lives. We enjoy life more when we find satisfaction in our immediate efforts rather than thinking how nice it is going to be when we finally arrive at our distant goal.

For example, we enjoy a road trip more if we decide to take an interest in the landmarks along the way rather than just enduring the ride until we arrive at our destination. Similarly, we enjoy a class more if we explore the content beyond what is required rather than doing the bare minimum to pass the class.

Do not make the mistake of setting unrealistic goals or having so many goals that it is impossible to reach them. Students frequently do this at the beginning of the semester. They soon become discouraged when they realize they have neither the time nor the energy to accomplish all of their goals. Recognizing our physical, mental, and emotional limits is an important component to realistic goal setting.

Changing Your Mindset

While some people are almost certainly going to be jealous as you start achieving your goals, your biggest obstacle is likely to be yourself. College students are often their own worst enemy, and for some reason, whenever we start to become successful, some primal defense mechanism kicks in, and our mind starts telling us all these crazy things – which we usually believe because, hey, we are a bit scared and afraid.

The truth is, we doubt just about everything along the path to success. Successful people are the ones who have tricked their minds into being supportive rather than critical, and although it takes some practice, you really can change your mindset so that you can get out of your own way. Here are some ways that you can make sure you have the right attitude as you chase down your dreams.

1. **Believe in Success**: One of the things that we all do from time to time is to convince ourselves that, for some reason, we do not deserve to be happy. Maybe it comes from feelings of guilt or perhaps just a lack of conviction that we are worthy of being happy and achieving our goals. Whatever the reason, if your mind is telling you that you do not deserve the

kind of success you're hoping for – remind yourself that the storyline is a lie. Believe that you deserve success and happiness. We all deserve it, but few people are willing to do what it takes to get it.

2. **Develop Confidence in Yourself:** You probably have heard the expression "Whether you think you can, or you think you can't… you're right." Confidence is a powerful thing, and when you have it, you are almost unstoppable, but when you lack it, it can be hard to accomplish anything. You truly can achieve your goals. You have the brains, the energy, the attitude, and the ability. You have every tool that you need to fulfill every single one of your desires. You need to do the work; the belief will follow.

3. **Avoid Thinking in Extremes:** Thinking in extremes – both positively and negatively – can become one of your biggest obstacles in life. We tend to think in very polarizing terms, up/down, on/off, success/failure, happy/sad, etc. Of course, none of these extremes are absolute, but it is hard to be objective about the full range of outcomes when you are standing right on the edge of something. Do not fall into the trap of thinking in extremes about your success or failures.

4. **Don't Overgeneralize**: Sometimes, we all can be drama queens when something bad happens. We say things like, "Oh, I'll never be able to achieve this goal." Negative thought processes are one of the worst mistakes you can make. Saying things like: "I must be the worst person ever to try this, I am not smart like other students." is a recipe for a long and difficult life. Setbacks are going to happen, and sometimes you are going to fail. It's not the end of the world, and you're probably doing better than a lot of people. Do not overgeneralize, try to look at things objectively, and, most importantly, keep going.

5. **Celebrate Your Success:** When you reach one of your daily, weekly, monthly, or yearly goals, don't minimize it. Achieving any goal is a big deal. Every single time you reach a goal – even if it's nothing more than your daily progress update – you are building momentum. Keep going, keep meeting those goals because before you know it, you will be achieving your dreams.

6. **Stop Believing Your Inner Idiot:** At times, we all allow negative thoughts to enter our minds, and somehow, we will start to believe these thoughts – or at a minimum, we start to behave in a manner that supports these negative thoughts until such time something happens to change that negative belief – and that is a sure way to lose your motivation. For example, suppose you have a calculus class this semester. Before you have even walked into the class, sat thru a few lectures, or read the first chapter, you might have convinced yourself that there is no way you will do well in this class. The class is just too hard, and you will probably end up lost by the end of the first week; you'll be pulling all-nighters to have any chance to pass…you get the idea. It is okay to think about what might happen in the future, but you have no idea what it holds, so don't convince yourself that you're a clairvoyant. You are not.

7. **Stop Thinking Perfection:** You are not perfect. You are never going to be perfect. No one on this Earth is perfect, and if you compare yourself to that standard, you are going to be the loser every time. Just accept that you are going to fail some of the time, and when you do, learn from it and move on. It is perfectly okay to strive for perfection as long as you never expect perfection. Each day strive to be the best version of yourself that you can be, but do not expect that version to be perfect.

Goals A Final Thought

As you can see, learning to structure your goals correctly and having the right mindset can make a big difference when it comes to your likelihood of accomplishing your goals. The key is to set your sights high but to have concrete, small steps that you can take along the way to get there. Don't focus on how long it is going to take. Deal with it being "boring" and focus on repeating the same few actions every day until you eventually achieve the thing you want to achieve or become the person you want to become.

If you assess the situation in the future after you have gained more experience and knowledge, you can rethink your approach again. Like anything else, this approach takes time, practice, and effort. In time, you will find things that work for you and things that don't work. You should make adjustments to your process as you gain more knowledge and experience!

Chapter 3:
Manage Your Time,
Manage Your Life

"Time = life; therefore, waste your time and waste
of your life, or master your time and master your
life." — Alan Lakein

When you start your college career, you have no experience in planning for your out of class coursework. A good rule of thumb is to schedule two to three hours of schoolwork outside class for every hour of class time. Yes, this means for a full-time student with five classes, a traditional fifteen-hour class load per week would have a baseline recommendation of between thirty and forty-five hours of study/homework time each week.

Sure, this is a lot of time, especially if you breezed through high school on a lot less. This estimate reflects the time it takes to learn effectively at the college level typically. The estimate is a general guideline; it's not a set-in-stone rule. Based on the difficulty of each of your classes, you can adjust your planned times up or down as needed. As I previously stated, in high school, about eighty percent of your learning was done in school, and only twenty percent outside of school. In college, the ratio is now reversed, creating a new challenge for you as a college student. You only do about twenty percent of your learning in class, and eighty percent of your learning occurs outside of class.

This change from a very structured high school environment to a highly unstructured college environment requires a completely different approach to your academic career. The key here is that you set aside this time exclusively for studying and then adjust based on your experience and results.

If you work a job and doing so isn't necessarily counterproductive to success at school, you'll need to consider your work schedule and make sure to plan some time for yourself each week. A starting point might be something like ten percent of your week or seventeen hours. What is more important than the specific targets is that you spend enough time on schoolwork to ensure that you're successful and that you spend enough time outside of school to ensure that you have a healthy balance.

Make sure you allow for unanticipated interruptions in your daily schedule. Leave some empty spaces during the day allows you to be flexible enough to handle interruptions or unexpected demands on your time that will happen. If the unexpected does not happen, time is available to do something else.

Many students find that if they schedule homework earlier in the day, they are less likely to be interrupted by unexpected events. Homework should be a part of each day's schedule. Students who participated in a major study on stress reported doing homework as the most frequently used method for reducing stress in their lives. That might sound odd to you, but by staying ahead of the curve and keeping homework done, your stress levels will be lower because you won't have that activity hanging over your head constantly.

Remember that your daily schedule should include at least some time for doing what you want to do rather than just a long list of "have-to-dos." Looking forward to something each day is good for our mental health and can help prevent the feeling of burnout. Some days may feel overwhelming when we look at our schedule. If this is the case, it is helpful to concentrate on one thing at a time and avoid looking at the entire day.

Inevitably, you will need to make adjustments to your plans and your time management habits. As you encounter time troubles, keep in mind that some are predictable, some are not; some are controllable, some are not. For those that are not controllable, keep your cool and get back on track as soon as possible. For time troubles that you can control, and particularly those that occur routinely, deal with them directly and quickly so that they don't prevent you from achieving your goals.

Time management requires self-management. It takes time, but after a short period of self-management, time-management becomes an everyday habit.

- Pay attention to how you spend your time.

- Do not procrastinate on chores to be done.

- Do not leave assignments and projects until the last minute.

- Schedule enough time in the day for doing things you enjoy and for eating and sleeping. Lack of sleep is an epidemic problem on most college campuses.

- Use your time wisely. If you take the bus or shuttle, plan to catch up on your reading while traveling.

One of the best time management strategies is staying one day ahead. I'm sure some collective groans meet this statement, but I promise that staying exactly one day ahead of your classes will make your life much easier, especially when that bug that is circulating campus knocks the wind out of your sails.

At the beginning of most of your classes, your professors probably will give you one of the most important pieces of information you will ever receive -- the syllabus. In high school, you probably never received a syllabus. You didn't know what the reading assignment or homework assignment was going to be in two weeks. In college, you do. Why is this important? It is the key to taking control of your time.

Let's say it's the very first day of class. You get your syllabus for your biology class. In most cases, the first day of class is a no-brainer -- often, a material lecture doesn't happen because the professor knows that a lot of people are going to drop/add classes that first week. You eye your nifty syllabus and see that the next class period will be a lecture over the first chapter of your $199.99 textbook. At this critical juncture, you may think:

"Wow, I already know what I'll be doing the next class period. I wonder if this is really valuable information. Could I use this to my advantage?"

Many students ignore the golden ticket of the syllabus, stuff it into their backpack, make a paper airplane, or find some other creative use for these sheets of paper and do nothing until the next class period.

When the next class period arrives two days later, you haven't read chapter one, but who cares because your professor is going to talk about it. You figure that you will use the time-honored tradition of taking notes in class. After all, everyone's doing it.

But if you're spending all of your time trying to copy PowerPoint slides or copywritten words on the board (your professor will most likely have handwriting that resembles some ancient language), you simply aren't going to absorb the material in most cases.

Let's say you take some great notes - good for you! Then you take the notes, which have all of the information you will ever need, and you put them in your folder, binder, backpack, or saddle-pack, and leave them there until the next lecture. Then you take more notes, add them to the pile, and soon you have lots of notes.

Before you know it, you have a test or quiz approaching, so you assemble your nifty notes and start restudying them like mad. You have to set apart a large chunk of time out of your schedule to review this old information so that it will be fresh in your mind for the test.

There is a better way. Now, let's pretend that you decided to get one day ahead. After your first-class period (and I know this is hard to do because, during the first week, there's so much fun to be found and so little work to do), you have a heart-to-heart with yourself and decide that you are going to get one day ahead.

If today's Monday, and the next class is Wednesday, you set aside some time on Monday afternoon or anytime on Tuesday and read the first chapter. You may even decide to take some notes, highlight, or even make notecards for definitions.

When you walk into class on Wednesday and your teacher starts talking, you have at least some idea and understanding around the lecture. You don't have to copy down definitions you've already read because you know they are in the book -- you remember reading them. Instead of frantically trying to copy notes like your poor confused classmates, you can relax and make a small tick mark to denote what the professor discussed and listen to what the professor is saying.

The lecture becomes your review session, and then you are in a much better position when test time comes. If the professor starts talking about something that you don't remember reading in the textbook, make certain to take good notes. The topic is either not covered in the book (so you can guarantee the professor will put it on a test), or it's something that you didn't quite absorb the first time you read it.

If you can do this for each of your classes at the very beginning of school, you will be in great shape. Once you get one day ahead, you can work at the same pace as everyone else, but always be a day ahead. Lectures will not be "note cramming sessions"; they'll be pseudo-reviews.

The toughest part is not getting lazy and letting that one-day buffer disappear. You can't let yourself slip behind because you know you're ahead. Once you lose that day, it's much, much harder to get it back in the middle of the semester because the pace of your classes will be picking up. If you can get ahead in that first week, the load will be much lighter.

Of course, there are exceptions to every rule. Not every class is equal in difficulty, and it may be extremely hard to get that one-day edge in certain classes that are complex or in classes that depend almost 100% on lecture material that doesn't come from a textbook.

Some classes may be just plain hard, and if you can't get a day ahead in one or two classes, that's fine. The time that you save by being ahead in your other classes will help you enormously in that tough calculus class you're taking.

If you find that reading your book is not helping you grasp the material, then talk to your professor. If they learn that you are trying to stay a day ahead, besides the inevitable brownie points that will follow, they will be willing to help you out. Professors are generally willing to bend over backward for any student that is putting out a serious effort to succeed in their class.

Let me mention that you may have some classes in which the professor has put together a "notes packet" that does contain copies of all the presentations and notes for that class. Be very careful not to depend solely on these notes as this could be a trap. Don't let those notes become an excuse to get lazy. Don't think that the class lecture doesn't matter because you have all the material, get one day ahead in the class notes, and again, all of the lectures will be your review sessions.

Pro Tip - Before arriving on campus, check your school's online portal to see if any of your professors have uploaded their syllabus. Some professors may expect you to come prepared to work on day one and may have already given you an assignment.

All these approaches will not guarantee your success at college. That's because everyone learns differently. Try some of these approaches and see what works for you, what doesn't, what needs to be modified. Also, please visit CollegeSuccessAcademy.com for more insights, recommendations, and training for college success. With that said, proper time management will have you well down the road to success with more time to enjoy your college experience than if you went down the traditional trial and error process of just plain winging it.

Putting the System into Action

Keeping a calendar is pretty straightforward, but surprisingly I have discovered most students don't keep one during their first semester or two. If they do keep one, it is usually just a class schedule with locations, so they know when and where to go until they get their routine committed to memory.

I am going to offer you some advice that seems counter-intuitive and conflicts with what most experts will tell you. First, let me say I am a fan of technology and using your Outlook, iPhone, or Google Calendar as a way to track your activities as most experts recommend, but I want this to be your secondary source of scheduling, not your primary.

I recommend the use of an Excel Spreadsheet, a DayMinder GC520 or similar planner, and your automated calendar during your first two semesters. I know this might sound like overkill, but the idea here is not to enter events and assignments into a calendar but to develop a system that keeps you organized and on track.

After a couple of semesters, you will find the system, and the process will have become a habit and will be natural for you.

Let's look at how all these approaches work together, and everything will become clear.

First Day/Week of the Semester

The first thing I want you to do is to take your syllabi from each class and markdown (in pencil) all your assignments for the semester in your DayMinder, don't forget mid-term and final exams).

Now use different color highlighters for each class (Math, English, Communications, Biology, etc.) and highlight your assignments in your planner.

Next, identify areas where you have multiple assignments, tests, exams, etc., all clustered together in a particular week or day. These clusters allow you to see clearly up front where you are going to be stressed and have little time. If you are like most students, you will see a convergence around spring and fall breaks and the last month of the semester. Take a deep breath and don't panic!

Now we want to pay attention to the weights of our assignments. Review your syllabi for each class and underline in red in your planner all your significant assignments. Significant is a subjective term, and each class will vary, but in general, anything that is weighted 10% of your grade or higher will qualify.

Once we have our core class schedule, we have to make some study estimates. Use two hours of study time for each hour of class time as a baseline requirement for scheduling your week. Adjust this baseline up or down based on your comfort and the difficulty of your class material. If you struggle with Math, you should bump up your baseline to three hours. If you are an English expert, you can adjust the baseline down to 1 hour or maybe 1.5 hours.

We now want to schedule our study time right into your planner. Planning a specific study schedule is key to avoiding procrastination. If you work or play sports and have that weekly commitment, schedule it now. Keep track of your study and assignment hours so that you can make adjustments throughout the semester. Things are probably starting to look pretty crowded at this point, and you are beginning to wonder where all that free time you heard about is going to show up. Don't worry. By planning, you will maximize your free time.

Now we want to identify the areas on your calendar where you have little or no assignments due. Highlight these areas in Green in your DayMinder or planner. These are the areas we are going to utilize to pull forward work you previously underlined in red and the areas where you have lots of things converging. Look for those large significant assignments and break them down into smaller chunks with new due dates you create for yourself; these are called milestones. By utilizing these green areas, you will balance your workload, ensuring you reduce future stress and have the time available to do your best work.

If you know you are going to go out with your friends on Friday and Saturday nights, make sure you schedule that time as well. If you are going to be out into the early morning hours and then sleep in until 2 pm, plan for that. Be realistic and don't set yourself up to fail by scheduling 4 hours of study time every Saturday morning when you already know you will be sleeping until early afternoon.

Now that we have everything organized and scheduled, we can enter everything into our online or smartphone calendars and set up our alert notifications. Our electronic calendars will now keep us on schedule, but our pre-planning ensures we effectively utilize our time.

I recommend that students get one day ahead in their classes as soon as possible. Things happen, schedules change, etc., but by building in a day buffer, you are preparing for that unplanned event that will inevitably occur at some point during the semester.

Also, class syllabi are guidelines, and the due dates and assignments will change in many instances. You will want to make sure you prepare for that new last-minute paper the professor decided to throw at you during the last month of classes. Yes, it happens more often than you will like. A professor will feel that the class isn't picking up on something as a whole or that something new has happened in the field, and the professor will decide to add an assignment to strengthen your academic foundation. He or She may feel like the class has not engaged or participated as well as they should have, or they may want to give everyone an opportunity to improve their grades. Regardless, you want to be prepared.

Also, schedule a time to Skype or call your family or someone else important to you back home. You will be surprised at how fast the days can run together, and although you are probably texting frequently, your loved ones love to hear your voice and see your face.

Here a link to a free template you can download and customize to keep your self-organized and on track.

http://collegesuccessacademy.com/index.php/schedule/

This template is very straightforward and easy to use and will summarize all your activities for you in one place (see table 1). You merely enter your activities on the Class List and Activities Tab (see table 2), classes, study time, practices, clubs, events, etc., in the tab, and the spreadsheet will organize everything for you.

Table 1: Time Management Schedule

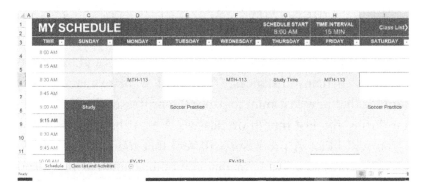

Table 2: Time Management Activities

Each Week – Review and Plan

Pick a day each week to review the week and month ahead. Most students find Sundays work best for this review. Remember to schedule calendar review time and treat this time like you would any other required commitment. Log into your university course management system (we use MOODLE at CCU) and review your upcoming assignment lists for any changes or assignments you may have missed. As a side note, make sure you confirm all assignments you turned in are showing as turned in.

Every semester students think they turned in an assignment, but the system will say otherwise. It is your responsibility to make sure your assignment was submitted and received. Use this time to clean up your email inbox and check and see if any of your professors have made schedule changes for the week ahead. The critical activity in this weekly review is to establish the specific activities and work you will perform during your allotted time slots.

Initially, we just blocked off the time we knew we would need. Once we have the specifics, we can now schedule the activities and tasks we need to complete during the week. As an example, we can take the three hours we have scheduled to study for a specific class and break down how we are going to use those three hours. Are we going to review note cards, read a chapter in the text, work on a paper, etc.?

Daily

Each day before noon, review your next day's schedule and school email account. If something new has popped up, you forgot about something, etc., by checking the next day's activities and your email early enough, you leave yourself time to course-correct if needed. Many students check their next day's calendar just before going to bed. If they have made a mistake or missed something, they have no time to correct their error, stress levels rise, they don't sleep, and the next day's performance suffers. Students often don't get emails sent to their university accounts regularly, so they can get out of the habit of periodically checking their school email and can miss valuable information such as assignments or cancellations of classes.

The Big Picture

Most students struggle with structure, and that is natural. By creating a schedule, you are not somehow magically sucking all the fun out of your life. In fact, you are reducing your stress and improving your performance, which will allow you to enjoy yourself a whole lot more. You will miss study sessions and other events on your calendar... that's ok. It is very valuable to know you missed an event and not go around fooling yourself into thinking you are on track. If you miss something, ask if you can make it up. You would be surprised how many students just assume the professor will not cut them a break. Make sure you identify what caused you to veer off course, make adjustments, and learn from the experience.

Creating Balance in Your Life

With everything that is going on in college, you need a simple system to make sure you have time for school, work, and fun. Yes, you're in college to get an education and to gain the skill you need for a successful career, but you also are here to have fun, create new experiences, and hopefully, a few lifelong friends.

There is a very simple technique you can use to make sure you keep your life in balance, a technique called *The Eisenhower Matrix or Eisenhower Box*. By utilizing this prioritization approach, you will be able to balance your hectic college life.

This useful technique is named after former President Dwight D. Eisenhower, who was the top general in World War II. He is credited with many accomplishments in his life, including leading the allied forces to victory, the development of the Interstate Highway System, and spearheading the creation of NASA. As a General and a President, he was widely regarded as extremely effective and organized. We all can learn a lot from President Eisenhower, so let's take a look at how he was able to accomplish so much. President Eisenhower was famous for saying, "What is important is seldom urgent, and what is urgent is seldom important."

The Eisenhower Matrix consists of a square which we divided into four sections or quadrants. Here's how the four quadrants are laid out:

We start by placing all our activities into the four quadrants, with the labels of Important and Urgent on each side. Each quadrant has a value of 1 through 4 based on their current priority.

1. **"Important" and "Urgent" tasks.** These are all your level 1 priorities. If you have an exam the next day, studying is probably a top priority. Paper due tomorrow, again, a level 1 activity, connect assignment due tomorrow, another level 1 priority. Level 1 priorities are those things with immediate deadlines, things that will make the most impact on your goals and vision, and these activities should grab your immediate attention.

2. **"Important," but "Not Urgent" tasks.** These are things still aligned with your goals and vision, but there is no immediate deadline staring you in the face. Maybe it is doing some extra reading on a topic in your major or attending a seminar before graduation, or reviewing your 4-year plan. You will work on these tasks whenever you have a lull in your schedule.

3. **"Not Important" but "Urgent" tasks.** These are things that you will complete after your level 1 priorities are complete or delegate altogether. Can your roommate check out that journal from the library for you? Could a friend pick up your toothpaste from the store for you? Maybe your parents need some information from you, or a friend needs a little help?

4. **"Not Important" and "Not Urgent" tasks.** These are the activities you put in quadrant 4, or activities you should eliminate altogether. Do you really need to binge-watch Season 3 of "Orange Is the New Black," or should you work on your quadrant 2 activities?

The underlying value in this matrix is its simple ability to compare activities, which activities are really urgent, and which are really important. Urgent activities will require your immediate attention; important activities help you with your long-term goals.

THE EISENHOWER MATRIX

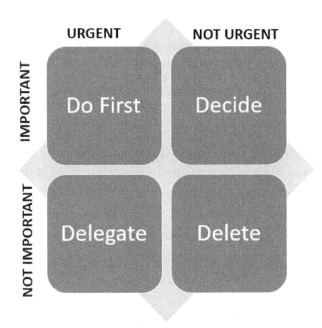

The Pomodoro Technique

When you prepare for a marathon, one of the best ways to increase your running mileage and run at a faster average pace or speed is to utilize the Run-Walk method during your training.

Developed by a world-renowned running expert, Jeff Galloway, the Run-Walk method requires you to run in cycles where you run for a fixed amount of time before walking for one minute and repeating the cycle as many times as needed to reach your target running mileage.

The logic behind this technique is that you give your legs the opportunity to rest to optimize recovery by taking short but frequent breaks instead of waiting until your legs feel like bricks before you rest them through walking.

The thing with this method is that you will have to slow down and walk for a minute at the end of your set running period, regardless of whether you feel tired or not. Taking short, regular breaks during the entirety of the run will help keep your leg muscles fresh for a much longer period, which enables you to run longer and faster.

The Pomodoro Technique is the mental equivalent of the Run-Walk method. It's a method wherein you work in cycles that are made up of a fixed number of work and rest minutes. This helps to keep your mind strong and fresh as long as possible, which will allow you to get more deep focus work completed.

The usual Pomodoro cycle involves 25 straight minutes of focused work, followed by a five-minute break, which you'll have to take regardless if you feel mentally exhausted or not. After every fourth cycle, you extend the break to ten minutes.

The point of the short and frequent breaks is to not let your mind reach total exhaustion before taking a break because if you wait, then it will be too late. By having your mind as strong and as fresh for as long as possible, you'll be able to extend your ability to focus on your work and block out the distractions.

Organization Matters

Usually, college students aren't quite prepared to organize all the "stuff" in their lives as they transition to college. Dorm rooms can quickly get overrun with stuff like clothes, books, computers, mini-fridges, microwaves, television sets, and the other possessions of the college student's life.

Even if you're going to college locally and still living at home in the same room you've been in since you were a child, you still need to make room for the new trappings of college life. Try a few of these organization tips.

You will need a few supplies to get you started. First, you will need colored file folders, a portable plastic file holder, some colored binders, a 3-hole punch, and a few small bins will get you started. Designate one color for each class and store pending assignments in them as you work on them. Place these folders inside the plastic holder. Be sure to write the class name on each folder for ease of identification. You can also use the file folder approach to store important papers and receipts.

The colored binders are used for each class to store all the papers you receive in that class. As we talked about earlier, you will get a syllabus – put this in the front. Then, whenever you get a handout from your professor, place it in the binder. Use section dividers to label what information corresponds with which section. You should also keep completed assignments in this binder for easy referral, and in case your instructor "loses" one of your grades – then you can prove you did the work! It does happen, especially when your professor is handling hundreds of student assignments at any given time.

Also, a professor may easily overwrite or enter a grade in the system wrong. Having an organized method to keep your assignments will make your life much easier when you sit down with your professor to review the mistake. You would be shocked to learn the number of times a student reaches out to me the last few weeks of the semester and asks for a copy of their initial assignment outlines, so they can get back to work on the project they were supposed to be working on all semester. Don't do this; it won't end well.

Keep on hand an ample supply of pens and #2 pencils, and use the bins for small items you accumulate like paper clips, push pins for a bulletin board, stapler, etc. It's a good idea to keep extra supplies like printer paper and printer cartridges – just in case!

Now that you have the tools, let's make sure you stay organized. Assignments can disappear in a pile of paper. Textbooks can get lost within a mound of laundry. A cluttered dorm room creates stress! Disorganization is all around us and happens practically everywhere, even in the most scholarly of places, like a college campus. But there is an easy solution.

The rule with paper is very simple. There are only three things you can do with paper:

1. Act on it

2. File it

3. Toss (recycle) it

For example, if you get a piece of mail, open it. Do not create a huge clutter problem by letting unopened mail pile up. You must decide what to do with your opened mail. If it is a catalog or a piece of junk mail and you know that you are not going to use, toss it. If it is a bill, pay it or mail it, or file it in a "bills due" folder. If you receive a memo or note, after reading it, toss it or file it away. If you get a paper returned, file it away. If you don't, clutter and stress will build.

Another important place to de-clutter is your computer. If you can keep your files under control, you will not be looking in 20 different folders in "My Documents" for that English paper you wrote last week. Here are some suggestions to get rid of computer clutter.

- Deleting or archiving any e-mail you read will keep your inbox clean.

- Create a filing system- if you cannot reply right away or need to save an e-mail, place it in a folder made for that category. (Needs Reply, or Archives)

- Watch your "sent mail" folder. Delete or archive things from that as well.

- Add to your address book often. Many times, people will keep an e-mail in their inbox so that they have the address for the future. Instead of that, save the address. You'll know where to find it later.

- Utilize spam filters on your e-mail account to limit inbox distractions. Just don't forget to check your junk and spam mail folder for things that slipped through.

- Setting up folders by semester will keep your "My Documents" folder easier to navigate, as well as allow for quick reference.

- Move files to Dropbox or another backup device as a standard course of business. You don't want to lose any work, and routinely back up your work in case of failure can save you untold time and stress.

Like any other skill, organization is a skill that can be learned. The most difficult part is breaking your lifelong bad habits. The key to getting better organized is to start with one small step and then take additional small steps one after the other. You may find that what you've put off for days takes only a few minutes to do. And once you see the benefits in one part of your life, you'll be motivated to expand this practice.

All the time management and organization tips in the world can only help if you put them to use. Putting things off can be the biggest mistake most college students make, so let's look at how you can get and stay motivated.

Chapter 4:
How to Get and
Stay Motivated

*"There will be obstacles. There will be doubters.
There will be mistakes. But with hard work, there
are no limits." — Michael Phelps*

There are plenty of articles, books, and blog posts on motivation that tell you how to become more motivated. Often, these resources just hit on the surface of motivation. These ideas are useful to an extent, but they ultimately fall short. If you struggle with motivation and cannot keep yourself focused on new tasks, then a tip or two isn't going to transform your ability to focus overnight.

And if you struggle to motivate yourself, how are you expected to keep up the changes that lead to greater motivation? It's something of a vicious circle, don't you think?

If you want to see changes, then you need to look a little deeper. You need to focus on the actual neuroscience that underpins our ability to get and stay motivated. In this chapter, you'll learn exactly how motivation works on a biological level, and more importantly, you'll discover how you can manipulate that process to your ends.

Introducing the Salience Network

What we're interested in here is what neuroscientists and psychologists refer to as attentional control or executive attention, which describes the ability we have to direct our attention and hold it – the power we have over what we choose to focus on and what we choose to ignore.

How does all this science stuff work in your brain? It comes down to several frontal regions within the brain that control our ability to focus. Perhaps most notable in the process is the anterior cingulate cortex, which lately has been the result of a fair amount of research.

It turns out; two separate networks or brain regions determine our brain's ability to concentrate: areas that work together to achieve the desired result. Specifically, these networks are known as the dorsal attention network, which includes brain regions that run along the top of the brain (dorsal means "top" in biology – hence "dorsal fin") and the ventral attention network (which runs along the bottom). Understanding these two different attention networks is key because they have different purposes that clue us in on how to get superior attention. The dorsal attention network is concerned with our intentional attention (a bit of a tongue twister). In other words, when you decide that you want to focus on your math book for a while, or you choose to check your smartphone, you are using the dorsal network.

When we find our attention reflexively directed beyond our control, that is the ventral attention network doing its job. In other words, when you hear a loud bang and you turn to look at it, that is your ventral attention network at work.

But your ventral attention network can also be distracted by a range of other biological clues. If you are hungry, for instance, then your ventral attention network will begin to direct your attention toward getting food, and if you are tired, then your ventral attention network will direct your attention toward rest. So, if you're trying to get work done and things keep distracting your attention, then it is going to be hard for you to maintain your attention!

The next question we need to ask is how the brain knows what should get its attention. The answer comes down to yet another neural network called the salience network. This network tells us what is important and what isn't, and it appears to connect closely to our ability to motivate ourselves.

In other words, those with the ability to tell their brain what is important will be able to stay focused on work, they'll be able to run longer distances, and they're able to stay intensely focused during competition. But what if you weren't born with a powerful salience network? What can you do to fix the situation?

Taking Back Control

The answer comes down to our evolutionary history. Every aspect of our psychology evolved the way it did to help us survive. Traits that proved conducive to our long-term survival would be passed on to our offspring, and those that did not would eventually die out.

Thus, the job of this network is to alert us to things that are important for our survival –biological signals from the body and our brain's associations trigger these alerts. If you see a bear, then your salience network will identify this as important, it will trigger the ventral attention network, and this will direct your attention there. The result will be that your parasympathetic nervous system kicks in and triggers a hormonal and neurochemical response: you'll produce adrenaline, dopamine, cortisol, and norepinephrine, and these chemicals will raise the heart rate, contract your muscles, and narrow your attention to that one thing.

To a lesser extent, this happens if you're hungry, too hot, too cold, or if you are experiencing stress about something else, whether that be your English class, an upcoming exam, a relationship, or anything else.

The first thing you need to do then to improve your ability to focus and stay motivated is to ensure that you remove these distractions that can override your dorsal attention network. To achieve the correct environment, you need to create a working environment that will be free from distractions and that makes you as comfortable as possible. Any loud noise, any discomfort, any hunger, or any lingering stress can potentially make it hard for you to maintain your focus.

One trick that you can use to encourage a more focused state of mind comes from WordPress creator Matt Mullenweg. He described to Tim Ferriss during a podcast interview how he would listen to music he knew well on repeat. The music would play over and over again, and he would become immensely familiar with it. As a result, the brain would then start to phase that music out. In other words, it would become desensitized to it, just as you eventually stop hearing the ticking of the clock. If you are listening to that music through headphones, it will drown out other noise.

By repeating music, you effectively create a kind of sensory deprivation. The only sound there is completely blocked out by the brain. You can achieve something similar by using white noise, and this is something that many people will use to focus while working. Similar to white noise are other innocuous sounds, such as the rain or background chatter. Rainymood.com and coffitivity.com are both sites that provide these kinds of looping sounds for you to block out your surroundings.

Another trick to help you stay focused while doing computer work is to use a widescreen monitor. Studies show that widescreen monitors can increase productivity by up to thirty percent. A 22-inch widescreen monitor has a productivity gain of about thirty percent over a 19-inch standard monitor. Productivity seems to peak with a 26-inch widescreen monitor, which further improves productivity by twenty percent over the 22-inch monitor.

One of the most important things you can do to maintain your focus is to try to remove all other stress from your mind. That means that you need to try and stop worrying about your GPA and even about the other work you have to do that day. If you are worried about those things, then your brain will keep being distracted away from what you need to do. So, try to learn to block out feelings of stress and anxiety and to focus on the task that is at hand. Blocking out distractions will take practice, but your brain is like any other muscle – the more you train it, the greater the control you will get over it.

Jedi Mind Tricks

But we need to go further than this if we're going to take complete control over our motivation. Ideally, we need to ensure that our ventral and dorsal attention networks are aligned. How do we do this?

The answer lies in the reason that we are distracted in the first place. The reality is not just that we think other things are more important at the time, but also that we feel what we should be doing isn't important or is just plain boring. You consciously might know that you need to study, go to the gym or library, but you are not feeling it. That's your dorsal network doing its work.

But your body doesn't know that. To your body, this is an unstimulating activity that isn't serving any of your prime directives. One thing our brain needs is stimulation, and that corresponds with a neural activity that comes from doing something that seems biologically important. Stimulation is why we find it easy to focus on video games, social media accounts, or YouTube – they simulate exciting, important events happening, all charged with emotion. Entering class notes into a Word document, though? Not so much.

But our human intelligence comes from our ability to focus not just on what is biologically important right now but on what we need to be doing in the distant future. In other words, we can extrapolate, plan, and predict, and that ability has made us highly effective.

The ability to understand the ramification of our actions comes from our working memory, which is our ability to store information in our "mind's eye," as it were. We can focus on things that have happened or things we think could happen, and this causes the brain to light up as though they are happening. The process we are experiencing is visualization – we're internalizing our experience to be able to manipulate the variables.

One way to give yourself more motivation is to learn to link the boring event or the thing you don't want to do to the worthwhile and important goal that you hope to achieve. In other words, you need to remind your brain why the task at hand is important. If you're typing out a spreadsheet, then visualize how this is going to eventually lead to you being wealthier, more successful in your career, and less stressed tonight. Consider what will happen if you don't do it – you will be behind with your classwork, and you won't be able to accomplish the goals you're aiming to achieve! If you're struggling to motivate yourself to go to the gym, then imagine what your life will be like when you're in great shape. Seem worth it now?

Another tip is to make whatever you're doing more interesting and more fun, which makes it more salient to your brain. I always say that the best cure for writer's block, in particular, is to make the scene or the paragraph you're writing more interesting. If it's not interesting enough to write, then it likely won't be interesting to read!

If you're doing data entry for a lab project, then make it a little more rewarding by putting the TV on in the background on mute – as long as it isn't too distracting to prevent you from paying attention to what you're doing. Oh, and once you get into the flow – make sure that there is nothing there to break that concentration. Put your phone on silent.

Master Your Brain

"The mind is the limit. As long as the mind can envision the fact that you can do something, you can do it, as long as you believe 100 percent." — Arnold Schwarzenegger

If you were to buy a car, a computer, a gaming console, or even a new tech device, then in all likelihood, it would come with an instruction manual of some sort so that you could find your way around its features and how you should use it. The user manual is important because it allows you to get the very most from your new purchase, and it allows you to avoid making mistakes that could damage it.

But unfortunately, the most important and most complex things in the world come with no such instruction manual. Take children; for example, any new parent will tell you just how dismayed they were when they realized that no one could tell them how to be an effective mother/father.

And then there's the big one, our brains. These are the most complex supercomputers in the entire world, and they are what create all of our subjective feelings, sensations, and experiences. And yet, our brains come with no instructions and no guidance: we are left simply to try and figure them out on our own. So, the question then becomes: How can you master your brain?

Fortunately, neuroscientists and psychologists are uncovering more of the brain's secrets every single day. While there is still a huge amount left to learn, we know more than we ever did, and a lot of this information can be used practically to help us become happier, smarter, and more effective versions of ourselves. Read on, and you will see how you can master your brain for complete and total self-mastery.

Neuroscience is a subject that can take decades to learn, and even then, it will be necessary to specialize in a specific area – as I said, it's a complex piece of machinery. There is much more than can be explained here, but we can nevertheless give a brief overview to give you some important clues as to how the brain essentially works. So, what do we know?

First of all, the brain is made up of neurons. These neurons are cells that have long tendrils called axons and dendrites. These reach out to almost touching each other, and that, in turn, means that they will be close enough for small signals to jump across the gap. In turn, creating a huge map made up of billions of neurons with incredibly intricate connections. This network is called the "connectome," and everyone's is slightly different. These individual differences are what give us our different skills and abilities and our different personalities.

These neurons are responsible for mapping every single experience that you have. Each neuron represents a sensation, a memory, an experience, a feeling, or something else. Your vision maps to a huge array of neurons that represent what you see, and likewise, your memory is made up of lots of interlinked neurons that reflect your thoughts and ideas.

These neurons are grouped roughly into different regions throughout the brain based on their function. In the occipital lobe, for instance, we have all the neurons responsible for our vision. In our motor cortex, we also have neurons that correspond with movements and sensations throughout our bodies. Our prefrontal cortex is where we handle things like planning and motivation. Our brain stem handles breathing. And our hippocampus stores many of our memories. The different regions of the brain explain why damage to one specific area of the brain can result in a loss of specific function, and this organization is so extreme that there have even been cases where a head trauma has led to a patient losing their memory in one area yet impacting no other areas.

Interactions between neurons occur through "action potentials." These are electrical impulses that occur once a neuron has received enough stimulation. That stimulation is normally the result of lots of nearby neurons firing enough to put it past a certain excitability threshold. When an action potential occurs, this can also result in the release of neurotransmitters. These are chemicals released from vesicles (sacs) that alter the way that neurons work– perhaps making them more or less likely to fire, or perhaps making the event seem more or less important/sad/happy/memorable.

Another factor that influences our differences is our balance of neurotransmitters and hormones. If you have lots of the feel-good neurotransmitter serotonin, then you will often be in a good mood, and you'll be relaxed. If you have lots of cortisol and glutamate, then you will be a more wired and panicked kind of person.

Neurotransmitters and Outside Influences

What's important to recognize here is that those neurotransmitters are not just a result of what is happening in the brain but can also be a result of biological signals from our bodies. For example, if you have low blood sugar, then your brain produces more of the stress hormone cortisol. Our body's evolutionary response is intended to make us seek out more food – but it is also the reason that we tend to feel anxious and angry when we haven't eaten for a while.

Conversely, serotonin can be released when we eat something and our blood sugar spikes. Serotonin is why we feel good when we've just eaten. That serotonin eventually converts to melatonin, which is the sleep neurotransmitter, and which suppresses neural activity. Melatonin is why we will often feel tired and sleepy after a big meal.

Countless other things also influence our balance of brain chemicals. Bright light, for instance, can reduce the production of melatonin and increase the production of cortisol and nitric oxide to wake us up. Remember: there were no artificial lights in the wild, and so our brain could rely solely on this signal to know what time of day it was! While there is much more to it than that, this very generally describes the form and function of the brain and how it gives rise to our individual experiences.

Brain Plasticity

Another aspect of the brain that is very important to familiarize yourself with is what is called plasticity. Brain plasticity (also called neuroplasticity) is the brain's ability to adapt and grow.

For a long time, we believed the brain only formed new neurons and new connections during childhood, and after that point, no growth occurred. However, we now know that this process continues until we die and is a crucial aspect of the way our brain functions. It does slow down slightly in adults, but it is still what gives us the ability to learn, to change our minds, and to acquire new skills.

Neural plasticity occurs through practice, repetition, and events that we believe to be very important. The saying among neuroscientists goes: "what fires together, wires together." In other words, if you experience something, a neuron will light up. If you experience that thing at the same time as another thing, two neurons might light up (or, more likely, two groups of thousands of neurons).

If you keep re-experiencing those two things together, a connection between them will begin to form. Subsequently, that connection will become stronger through a process called myelination, during which the dendrites and axons become insulated to conduct the flow of electricity better. Eventually, one neuron firing will cause the other neuron to fire. Neurons firing allows you to learn a complex series of movements when dancing, or how you can memorize words in a new language. At this point, I am sure the question you are having is how you can productively use this information?

Controlling Neurotransmitters

One way to hack your brain for greater productivity, happiness, or whatever else, is by influencing the production of neurotransmitters. We've learned that these influence our mood and our ability to learn, so changing the balance of these chemicals could certainly be very useful.

Neurotransmitter balance is why a lot of people are interested in the idea of nootropics. Nootropics are smart drugs, supplements, and medications that can influence the production of neurotransmitters so that we have more goal-oriented dopamine or less fear-inducing cortisol. Modafinil alters the production of orexin, which can completely change our sleep/wake cycle, so we feel more awake. Influencing balance is also what caffeine does, by removing the inhibitory neurotransmitter adenosine (or neutralizing it, to be more precise).

The problem with this strategy is that it fixes the brain into a specific, unnatural state and prevents you from being able to easily switch modes. No one brain state is superior to all others – for example, creativity requires relaxation, not stimulation.

Worse, the brain can adapt to those changes by creating more or fewer receptor sites (the points where the neurotransmitters work) to make us more or less sensitive to the neurotransmitters in question. An overdependence on an unnatural brain state can eventually lead to addiction.

Some of our neurotransmitters do work better by focusing more on neuroplasticity or more on energy production, but for the most part, this is not the solution.

What is a much more useful solution is for us to look at those factors that naturally influence neurotransmitter release and balance. If you want to hack any system, you need to understand what the inputs are.

We know that bright light can increase energy and make us less sleepy. Why not consider investing some money in a daylight lamp which is designed to combat SAD (Seasonal Affective Disorder) by simulating the sun's rays? We know that cold likewise can increase focus, while heat can help us to feel more relaxed and happier. We know that the sun and that exercise can boost our mood through the production of serotonin.

We also know that our brain is subject to certain natural cycles, those relating to sleep and hunger, for instance. By timing our productivity around those things, we can work more effectively and free from distraction.

And if you find yourself feeling very stressed or depressed, then it might pay to consider some of the biological factors that may be causing that. Perhaps you're hungry? Or perhaps you're a little ill, and the pro-inflammatory cytokines are causing brain fog? Once you know the problem is transient and biological, it can be much easier just to let it pass.

Controlling Your Brain

It is critical that you learn to create the moods and the feelings that you need by changing the way you think and use your brain.

The thing that makes humans unique is our ability to visualize – to internalize events and to imagine future scenarios or possibilities. Visualization is our working memory at play, and it is what enables us to think of long-term goals and to invent new ideas. And if you believe in the theory of embodied cognition, then you might find that this is what we use to understand plain English (look it up – it's very fascinating!).

When we visualize or imagine, we do so by lighting up the same neurons in the brain as though the event were happening. Neurologically, we find doing something and imagining doing something almost indistinguishable.

Given this known neurological response means that you can use visualization to practice things and develop skills – you can trigger brain plasticity just as though you were practicing the event! Not only that, but you can also use this as a way to trigger the appropriate neurotransmitters to put yourself in the correct state of mind.

Ultimately, this will lead to the ability to control your own emotions – to trigger the best possible mental state for the task at hand. It requires training of your visualization skills and the awareness to use those skills to ease your anxiety and to motivate yourself to focus and to become more alert as necessary. Managing your emotions is the neuroscience that underlies psychological approaches such as cognitive-behavioral therapy and philosophies such as stoicism.

It is also important to avoid bad habits – even bad habits in our thoughts – as ruminating and indulging strengthens connections that make those habits harder and harder to break.

There's a lot more to making the most from your brain, but I hope this basic primer has given you a better understanding.

Chapter 5
Overcoming
Procrastination

"The only difference between success and failure is the ability to take action." – Alexander Graham Bell

It Takes Time

Some people must overcome procrastination gradually. Almost no one has trouble studying the night before a big exam. But without the pressure of an exam, many students find it easy to avoid studying. The key is to learn the habit of getting started on a task early. The procrastinator needs to learn to initiate studying and preparing for papers and exams well in advance. Practice starting to study several times every day. As with exercising, getting started, and making it a routine are the secrets to success. Other valuable suggestions to get you going include:

- Recognize self-defeating problems such as fear and anxiety, difficulty concentrating, poor time management, indecisiveness, and perfectionism.

- Keep your goals in mind and identify your strengths and weaknesses, values, and priorities.

- Compare your actions with the values you feel you have. Are your values consistent with your actions?

- Discipline yourself to use time wisely.

- A study session that utilizes small blocks of time with frequent breaks is more effective than studying in long uninterrupted marathon sessions. For example, you will accomplish more if you study/work in sixty-minute blocks and take frequent ten-minute breaks in between than if you study/work for two to three hours straight, with no breaks.

- Reward yourself after you complete a successful week.

- Motivate yourself to study. Focus on success, not on failure. Try to study in small groups. Break large assignments into smaller tasks. Keep a reminder schedule and checklist.

- Set realistic goals.

- Modify your environment: Eliminate or minimize noise/ distraction. Ensure adequate lighting. Have the necessary equipment at hand. Don't waste time going back and forth to get things. Don't get too comfortable when studying. A desk and a straight-backed chair are usually best (a bed is no place to study). Be neat! Take a few minutes to straighten your desk.

- Decide when you have had enough, and it's time for a change.

- Think about the activities that you use to procrastinate (email, TV, etc.) and set clear time limits on them.

- Set clear goals for each day (e.g., start CHEM problem set, do ENGL reading, finish MRKT chapter reading), and stick to them. Once complete, you are free to do whatever you like.

- Remember that serious academic stress usually follows procrastination.

- Recall the stress and loss of energy you felt the last time you had to stay up all night to write a paper or study for an exam.

Remembering your feelings of anxiety can serve as an effective motivator to help you get started on time now.

• Know that overcoming procrastination is sometimes easier if you talk out strategies for change with someone else.

If the volume of work on your to-do list overwhelms you, you might benefit from making a "one-item list." Re-write the top item from your list at the top of a blank page and work the task to completion, then take the next item on your list and place that on a blank sheet, repeat the process until you complete everything on your original list.

Aim to subdivide tasks into small steps and convince yourself that to get started, all you need is five minutes working on the task. Often, the five minutes is all you'll need to get into the swing of things, and you can continue productively. I call this trick "The Five-Minute Hack."

Try working for a short time, and see if you can "get into it." If your motivation problem seems more substantial, it might help to realize that when you aren't motivated to do schoolwork, you aren't out of motivation... **you are just motivated to do something else.**

Make every effort to develop the discipline you need to follow your plan. Your planner should always be handy, and you should refer to it often. Once you make your schedule, follow it. If you need help staying on task, work with a roommate or friend to motivate each other and hold each other accountable. Remind yourself you are focused on your long-term goals, and once you complete your work, you are one step closer to achieving those goals. And remember, by sticking to your plan, you will have more time for yourself.

If you are struggling to stick to your plan, try this tip. Make two activity lists: "Things I Like to Do" and "Things I Have to Do." Mix up activities from both lists and work on each activity for a short period. Alternating between fun activities and work helps to maintain motivation and interest. All work and no fun is another schedule buster. You don't have to be working ALL the time, but you do have to complete what is required to stay on plan.

Sometimes, you're going to feel overwhelmed with large projects or assignments. Remind yourself that this is a normal reaction. When you feel like this, it's easier to put things off because you don't know exactly where to start and have a difficult time envisioning the completed task. Divide these major assignments into smaller parts and work on one part at a time. Then put them together into the whole project and feel the satisfaction of a job well done!

You might have every intention of doing things promptly, but time can move swiftly. There are only 24 hours in each day, and some students are just over aggressive with their planning. Make sure your schedule is realistic, and you aren't involved in too many activities scheduled close together. If you spread yourself too thinly, none of your projects will get the attention they deserve. Reward yourself when you complete tasks on time. Make the reward appropriate for the difficulty and boredom of the task. Utilizing rewards will help you stay on task and provide fuel for action.

Remember that you're not alone. Some studies report that up to 95% of college students experience procrastination as a real problem. Many students do most of their work in marathon sessions near academic deadlines and they fail to make appropriate use of time management skills, tools, and tips I recommend. Doing this leads to more stress in your already stressful life. Why add to your stress?

Keeping it Simple

When it comes to a habit of procrastination, tasks and projects that are complex and ambiguous can make it harder for even the most disciplined of people to avoid procrastination. Simple plans of action and expected results are much easier to understand and implement. Also, plans that are easier to understand and implement are plans that are at low risk for procrastination, that is, unless you are already a habitual procrastinator.

You can look at it this way, are you more likely to procrastinate when you have the task of making a cake for your sorority bake sale that you'll have to bake yourself, even if you have previous experience baking, versus when you have to order a customized cake from an online bakeshop to present to your sisters? Chances are pretty high that you'll procrastinate on baking a cake yourself because it is more complex and complicated compared to ordering a custom cake online. The mere thought of having to find the perfect recipe, buying all the ingredients, and actually baking the cake can be enough to make you put off doing it until the last minute.

Talk to Yourself

To beat procrastination, you have to use positive self-talk. If you don't know how to start positive self-talk, here are a couple of useful ways to get you started. First, you can use positive affirmations or declarations to help you overcome bad habits like procrastination. You may be wondering how this works exactly.

The human mind controls how you behave and act, but there are two aspects of the human mind that account for different kinds of behaviors. There's the subconscious mind, which regulates many of your actions, especially those that you're not aware of but are important, like breathing, your heartbeat, your ability to walk. All the actions that require conscious thought or awareness, like solving a math problem, writing an essay, and eating a meal, are all controlled by your conscious mind.

Habits, like procrastination, are unconscious, and they fall under the control of the subconscious mind. This is the reason why you can only go so far when trying to consciously change your habits before you revert back to your normal habits. This includes things like smoking, cursing, and procrastinating. The only way that you can make lasting personal change is by converting them into habits, either subconscious or conscious, through reprogramming your subconscious mind.

According to Dr. Maxwell Maltz, the author of *Psycho Cybernetics*, the subconscious mind can be likened to heat-seeking or laser-guided missiles launched from fighter jets and warships. When these kinds of missiles are launched, they automatically seek out the targets given to them. After the missiles are launched, the pilots and warship captains no longer have control over the movements or trajectories of the missiles. The missiles' on-board computer systems are what control them en route to their programmed targets. The best way to control these kinds of missiles is to give them their targets before they're launched.

Your subconscious mind is like these guided missiles. You can make it go wherever you want and achieve what you want by simply programming it to acquire certain targets or habits, like eating healthy, exercising, and ending procrastination. You can do this by using your conscious mind through visualization and affirmations or through declarations and positive self-talk.

To help you retrain your subconscious mind and end procrastination, you need to say your positive declaration several times a day and with emotion. An example affirmation might be, "I will stop procrastinating and, instead, be a very proactive person." When you continually tell yourself this, you can change your subconscious mind's programming over time so that it will manifest the affirmation. It can even become more powerful if you combine it with visualization exercises, where you play a movie in your mind's eye, and you see yourself acting or living out your affirmations.

Another way you can use positive self-talk to reprogram your subconscious mind and end procrastination is by asking the right questions, particularly positive and empowering ones. An example of the right question to ask would be, "What should I do to start getting ahead in my classes?" rather than "Why am I not able to ever get ahead in my classes?"

By asking how you can achieve something rather than why you can't, it allows your subconscious mind to focus on how you can. When you ask why you can't achieve something, you are effectively programming your subconscious mind to continue keeping you from successfully accomplishing something or getting rid of a bad habit.

What you focus your mind on often determines, to a great extent, how your subconscious mind will be programmed. If you can program your subconscious mind for the possibilities, it will go after those possibilities. If you program it for limitations, it will do what it can to enforce them.

Reward Yourself

The first thing to do to keep you motivated with your work is to come up with your own rewards for completing an assignment. For example, getting a bowl of ice cream or your favorite snack while working can serve as a reward. Every time you finish working on a problem area, you can eat a part of the snack. This way, you will be motivated to continue working forward just to have a taste of that small reward.

Find An Accountability Buddy

The second thing you can do to make sure you stay motivated is to ask another student to check up on you. The support of this person, making sure that you are alright and that you are on track, will help to pressure you to continue working. It will motivate you to ensure that when he returns to see what you have been doing, you can show him that you have actually been working successfully. On the other hand, it is like having your professor walk in randomly and seeing that you have not accomplished anything.

Be Accountable To Your Own Actions

The third thing that can be done is to determine and carry out an unpleasant consequence for not doing the task. You can take away the rewards you have set for yourself or spend more time at the computer working instead of walking outside. Basically, instead of taking a break and relaxing in the middle of work to reward yourself for getting so much done, you will sit there and continue working because you are punishing yourself for relaxing when you should have been working hard.

Weigh & Seek Out Your Best Options

The fourth thing that can be done is to work out the cost of the time you have utilized and think about how this cost will impact your future. College is expensive. Having to take a class over again because you procrastinated and failed to obtain a passing grade is even more expensive. Graduating in five years instead of four not only adds to the cost of college but costs you a lost year of earnings. Over the course of your working career, an extra year or two of college could cost you upward of $300,000 in lost work and investment income.

If you are a person who procrastinates because you are disorganized, then the above tips, which aim to stop procrastination, will not be sufficient for you to overcome your procrastination habit. You will need to adopt some strategies and tools that will allow you to get organized.

Schedule A To-Do List

I am not a fan of the traditional To-Do List. Advocates of this approach believe if you write down a simple to-do list of daily tasks, this will ensure that nothing is forgotten and that you will magically be driven to complete everything on your list, no matter how unpleasant or overwhelming the tasks are. This approach simply doesn't work for procrastinators.

In order for a To-Do List to work effectively, the list must be prioritized and actually scheduled in your daily planner. The procrastinator must become a master scheduler.

Set Priorities

Take your To-Do List and look and arrange the tasks from the most important to the least. Doing the things that are most important first will produce the best outcome for the day. Once this task is done, you should remember that other things still need to be done, but they are not as important at the moment.

Scheduling & Project Planning

The key to overcoming procrastination is to become better at scheduling and project planning. Once you realize that you will have plenty of time for fun activities once you complete your work, the actual work will seem less painful, less stressful, and thus your emotional need to avoid the work in the first place will be diminished. Once you know exactly when to start your projects and tasks, you become more relaxed, and you are freed up to perform your best work.

Set The Time Required To Complete Each Individual Tasks

The next thing you can do is set a certain amount of time for each item on the list. You should be able to make an estimate as to the amount of time you will need to complete a task on the list. For example, reading a chapter in your English book might only take an hour, while completing an entire paper might take days. Ensuring that you can work within the allocated time and working on your priorities will not only help you to stay on schedule but will ensure you achieve your best results.

The most important thing to do is to focus on one task at a time. If a task becomes too overwhelming or if you are seeing too much on the list, try to break things down into smaller chunks or work units. This will help you to create a better plan, which will allow you to continue working and rewarding yourself instead of just stopping altogether for the rest of the day.

Chapter 6:
How Successful People Overcome Procrastination

"Focus on being productive instead of busy." Tim
Ferriss, author, and entrepreneur

Productivity is often a misunderstood concept. Being productive isn't necessarily about accomplishing more, but rather it's about investing your time and attention in a more strategic way to add value to your education, life, and relationships. If you're like most people, you probably wish that you could be more productive in your life. However, one thing that you may have failed to consider is the reason and motivation that drives you to work toward accomplishing your goals.

Too often, our desires to be more productive are based on the belief that it is what is expected of us by our parents, our professors, our employers, and society. Sometimes all students may feel the need to be productive because they are overloaded with classwork and don't feel like they can handle their class workload. While these are all valid reasons for wanting to be more productive, they are all external reasons.

Other external motivators for wanting to be more productive may include material things, money, or fame. While money can be a great motivator for many people, it is vital that you consider whether there is something else driving you. If your reasons for wanting to be more productive are shallow ones that don't serve a higher purpose in your life, chances are high that it will ultimately decrease your motivation.

If you want to increase your productivity, then you need to take the time to consider what is driving your desire for productivity. If you need more money to support your family, then the love you have for your family might be your driving factor. Perhaps, you have found yourself in poverty, and your drive is the desire to improve your situation and yourself. If you want to improve your productivity, you need to determine what drives you on a deeper level and understand why you are working so hard.

It is critical that you make sure that you know what you are striving to achieve. Only you know what is driving you. Only you know what will make you wake up early and work hard. Only you know why you need to be more productive. If you are going to college because it just seems like the thing to do or your parents have made you do it, being productive is going to be a problem.

It does not matter what you tell other people, and it doesn't even matter if it's true or not. If you tell people what they expect to hear, but what you say conflicts with your true feelings, this conflict will be counterproductive. What does matter is what you tell yourself? If you want to improve your productivity, you have to be honest with yourself. To keep your productivity from falling as quickly as it has risen, you need to continue to remind yourself why you are working so hard, being sure to always keep it in your heart and mind. If you want a college degree so you can take care of your parents, grandparents, kids, or provide for your future, you need to keep that desire front and center.

Unfortunately, there is not a magic pill that you can take to fix your procrastination and overall lack of productivity. Improving your productivity is going to take your time and hard work, and you will have to change how you work before you can see a permanent boost in your productivity.

Exceptional People You Likely Never Heard Of

Sure, we all know about the exceptional productivity of Elon Musk, Bill Gates, Oprah, and other famous people. But there are plenty of examples of productive people all around us; these people have no special productivity gene. What makes them exceptional is the fact that they were able to overcome procrastination, and this achievement enabled them to go farther in life. They used to have the tendency to push off assignments and continue waiting until the last few minutes to get everything done. They noticed what was happening and decided to put a stop to it. The best part is that they decided to share their experiences by writing these tips, aiming to help other people succeed. To specify, these people are coaches, authors, productivity experts, entrepreneurs, and bloggers. It is said that success leaves clues, and we can shorten our learning curve and accelerate our results from modeling the success of others. So, with that said, let's look at a few people who overcame their procrastination to live the life they wanted to live.

Mike Vardy

Mike Vardy is an excellent productivity strategist and the founder of Productivityist. He overcame procrastination by utilizing a simple strategy of attaching a kind of "mode" (work mode, play mode, sleep mode, exercise mode) to every single task he faced. Once he was in a certain mode, he was able to stop himself from pushing away the task and just do it right on the spot. Every time he had a task in front of him, he continued with it because he was in the right mode or mindset at that moment. This was just the beginning of his success when it came to overcoming procrastination.

Continuing with his desire to improve his productivity, he learned about the relationship between a task and the amount of energy required to complete a task. Tasks that require a low or high amount of energy are perceived differently by the brain. An important assignment that requires more focus and effort because it takes longer to do will demand a higher amount of energy to complete it. By aligning your tasks with your energy levels, you will naturally maximize your efficiency. For example, you can choose to work on bigger, complex, or challenging assignments when your energy is at a peak and leave the simple stuff for periods of lower energy. Let's face it, some tasks are easier to do in the morning versus the evening based on how awake or how relaxed you are throughout the day.

Darren Rowse

Darren Rowse is the founder of ProBlogger. He overcame procrastination by designing his own weekly schedule. He started by listing the activities which needed to be done throughout the week. Then, he organized them by determining which tasks had to be accomplished on a specific day within that week. These tasks were then placed in order of the amount of energy it would take to do them and how important they were, depending on which day of the week it was.

Sometimes, there were tasks that had to be completed by Tuesday, while others had to be handed in by Friday. If there were three assignments that had to be submitted by Tuesday, then the tasks which took the most amount of energy to complete were prioritized. Darren ordered his tasks by determining the amount of energy it would take to complete them. This strategy made him realize that it was better to complete his tasks in two days instead of just one. From there, he set a goal for himself to complete these tasks within a certain amount of time during the day. As a result, he was able to design a schedule that stopped procrastination in its tracks. He points out that the key to being efficient in accomplishing quality work is knowing how to prioritize the tasks in your schedule.

Erik Fisher

Up next is Erik Fisher. He is the author and productivity podcaster of Beyond The To-Do List. He found that the best way to avoid procrastination is to be ready to say "no." Apart from doing tasks which you are able to do, it is equally important that these tasks are something you really want to do. When taking on an assignment that is not so interesting, it is easy to wait until the last minute before acting on it because you simply do not want to do it.

When an exciting assignment arises, it is much easier for you to complete it earlier on in the week. Also, it is easier to make time for it and set it as your task of the highest priority for that day. On the other hand, after setting up a long list of tasks that should be completed within a certain amount of time, sometimes it is still difficult to sit down in front of a computer and truly work on an assignment that is scheduled to be done during that time.

The second step, which Erik mentioned about beating procrastination, is to break down each task into the smallest number of sections as much as possible. Breaking down projects this way will make it more manageable for you to complete them. Therefore, you can slowly reward yourself for getting past another step. This strategy will make your tasks less overwhelming, and it also makes them more plausible to complete in a faster amount of time.

Tony Stubblebine

Tony Stubblebine is the CEO and founder of Coach.me. He broke through his procrastination struggles by using basic meditation and by understanding that it is an obstacle that needs to be overcome. He viewed this scenario as a challenge to control his thoughts and to control what he was doing throughout the day.

Meditation taught him different and higher levels of awareness and control, which helped him to stay focused on everything that had to be done. He describes procrastination as something that happens in the subconscious level of the mind. It is through focus where a person will be able to see how much he can accomplish towards a single assignment. Tony realized that he needed to face his mental battle to fight procrastination head-on.

Chapter 7:
Focus and Productivity

"You miss 100% of the shots you don't take." Wayne Gretzky, HOF
professional ice hockey player.

Don't Be Afraid To Say NO!

Darren Hardy tells a great story about Richard Branson. As the story goes, a Fortune 500 company had hired Darren as a speaker for their big corporate retreat. The CEO of the company told Darren that they were trying to get Richard Brandon as a speaker for their event, but they were having trouble getting in touch with Mr. Branson.

Darren told the CEO that he and Richard were friends, so he would try to connect the two. The CEO told Daren that he would pay Mr. Branson $100k for an hour and a half talk.

So Darren got in touch with Richard's office, and he told Richards's assistant to relay the offer to Mr. Branson. The message back was to let the CEO of the company know that Richard was unavailable to speak.

The CEO was not deterred. He says, "We really want Richard at our event! Call them back and let them know we will pay $250,000!"

Darren makes the offer… and once again, the offer is rejected!

He calls the CEO and gives him the bad news. Now clearly upset, the CEO instructs Darren to call them back and offer $500k for a 1-

hour speech, and we'll send our private jet to pick him up and immediately take him back to the plane after the speech!

Darren calls Richard's office... he is once again turned down. He then asks what it will take to get Richard to come to do the speech?

The reply, "Richard currently has 3 Strategic Objectives that he is working on... and a paid speaking engagement is not one of those Strategic Objectives!"

The difference between average and great is often a simple matter of focus! Take a lesson from Sir Richard Branson and create your own list of goals. Narrow it down to a top three, and then do not focus on anything else until it is completed!

Pizza and Success?

Each semester I ask my students how many of you would make a 4.0 this semester if I gave you $1 million dollars for achieving that target. Every hand goes up. So why do so few students actually make a 4.0 and get on the President's List? The simple answer comes down to focus and priorities.

If we focus our efforts 100 percent on one thing, we will have a high probability of achieving success. Of course, with all our efforts focused on only one thing, we likely will alienate those around us, and this extreme focus will likely leave us feeling empty and unfulfilled. We may graduate we a great GPA, but we missed out on a well-rounded college experience.

100% Focus On One Thing - High Probability Of Success

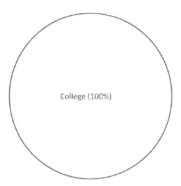

If we focus our efforts on two things, college and work, we still have a high probability of success, but we still will miss out on all the networking, and social benefits college has to offer.

50% Effort On Two Categories – Probability of Success Still High

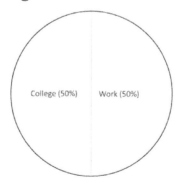

Now, say we can focus our efforts on four categories, college, work, fun, and self-care, we can have a well-rounded college experience and still have an average chance of meeting all our goals.

25% Effort 4 Categories – Probability of Success Average

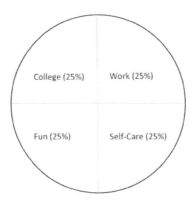

The real problems kick in when our efforts and focus start on looking like a bunch of thin slices of pizza. When our energy and focus are spread so thin into a bunch of small slices, our chance of success becomes very poor.

When Your Focus Starts To Look Like A Pizza - You Have A Problem!

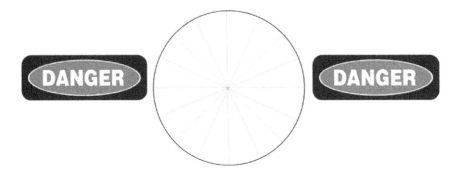

Keep your circle of focus as clean as possible. Richard Branson likes to say if you have more than three or four areas of focus, you have no focus. Get clear on who you want to Be and become relentless in the pursuit of who you want to Be, and you will have everything you want to have.

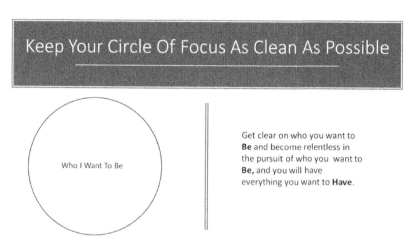

You see, ninety-nine percent of the population has it backward. They focus on what they want, not who they have to become to achieve what they want to achieve. Maybe you want to attract an amazing spouse. Ask yourself, what characteristics and traits would attract an amazing spouse? Then simply go to work, becoming that type of person.

Mental Focus

Mental focus is the ability to concentrate on a single task or project without getting distracted. Learning to focus better and for longer periods of time on any task, project, or goal will help you get more done in a lot less time, do higher quality work, and become more successful not just in college but in life.

Mental focus is one of the most important skills when it comes to success in college. To focus means to concentrate on a particular task or problem for a period of time. Can you focus on a complete 50 minute long lecture? Work on your paper for two hours without distractions? Study for that exam for four hours without checking out mentally every five minutes. Like any skill, focus is something you have to practice to improve.

Focus Keeps Distractions At Bay

Distractions are all around us. You sit down at your desk and end up checking your email, browsing through Instagram, or getting lost on YouTube watching silly video after silly video. We get distracted by roommates, our surroundings, even our own thoughts. With all these distractions, it's a wonder we get anything done. There's always something else that demands our attention or a fun new thing we'd rather give our attention to.

This is where focus can make a huge difference in your life and help you get the right things done. Focus is like a pair of blinders. It helps you concentrate on the task at hand until it is done and done right!

Focus Keeps You From Making Mistakes

The great race car driver Mario Andretti was asked for his best advice for becoming a world-class racing champion. His response was quite surprising. He simply said, "Don't look at the wall." He then added that your direction will follow what you focus on, so if you look at the wall, you will probably hit the wall! Sound advice whether you are traveling at 200 miles per hour or trying to get your college degree. The best approach to success is to get clear on what you want and keep your eyes on the priorities that will get you there.

Because you are not constantly distracted and you are giving your full attention to whatever it is you are working on at the moment, you're less likely to make mistakes or errors of omission. Mistakes happen when your attention is divided, and you are not fully engaged and immersed in the task you are working on, and subsequently, you miss things.

Being focused, on the other hand, helps you concentrate on your work and things like your class lecture. It allows you to take better notes, which leads to making fewer mistakes because you processed all the information initially, and when you do make a mistake, if you're not distracted, you're that much more likely to catch it and fix the error. The end result is not just better-quality work but improved efficiency no matter what you're working on.

Focus Helps You Get More Done Faster

Most students find themselves working on tight deadlines. Let us say you must finish a report before you can head out to class or to meet a friend. If you are highly focused (thanks to that looming deadline), a task that would usually take you half a day is suddenly accomplished in an hour. When you are highly focused, you are getting into the flow where everything just comes together almost effortlessly.

Mental Focus In College Is Essential To Your Success

In today's busy college life, being self-motivated and focused is becoming more and more important. It doesn't matter what major you're in. You have to be able to focus and show results without your parents' supervision, a detailed assignment review, or a teacher that spells out each step of your task for you.

When you are working independently, particularly in the library or your own dorm, it's easy to get distracted. Most of our work is now done on our computers, where sites like Facebook, Instagram, Snap, and YouTube are a constant source of temptation and distraction. Being able to focus on the things you need to get done will help you get your work done in a timely fashion, and it gives you a leg up on other students who may not be as focused as you are.

Increase Your Focus For Better Productivity

In our modern lives today, we are busier than ever before. We think technology has streamlined many tasks, but instead, we are given more tools that give us more and more to do with less time to do it. We are stressed and overwhelmed. The phrase "time management" has become front and center, as it implies there are even more ways to cram even more into our already overflowing lives.

We have been led to believe that if we don't multitask every minute of our day, we will not be productive. This can't be farther from the truth. Successful people have long realized that focus is the key to being productive.

Most of what we say and do is not essential. If you can eliminate it, you'll have more time and more tranquility. Ask yourself at every moment, 'Is this necessary?' ~Marcus Aurelius

Increasing your focus means you should get up each day, looking forward to what you can achieve. Being focused means, you are making progress towards what is most important to you. With improved focus, you will feel a greater sense of productivity and fulfillment.

In this chapter, you'll learn the key tips and strategies on gaining and keeping your focus so you can be productive in everything you do. Let's get started.

Why Focus Is Important

Why is being focused so important in today's world? What results happen when you are focused? Does being focused make you less stressed? Happier? If focus so important, why don't people focus more?

Being focused on one thing for a certain period of time allows you to do a better quality of work, more work gets done quicker, and your creative ideas flow easier. Being focused on one task at a time is less stressful on your mind. And being less stressed allows you to be happier.

It's difficult for students to remain focused on one task for a variety of reasons. For one, we live in a world where we are constantly bombarded with TV, radio, cell phones, social media, as well as the fact that in dorms, we have many students living virtually on top of each other.

It's difficult to get completely away from all these distractions. One way is to find a spot where you can get some privacy and turn off your phone and email notifications.

- When you focus on a single task, avoiding distractions, your brain becomes focused on that task alone. This lets you complete that task much more quickly than if you are trying to complete two or more tasks at once. For instance, let's say you need to write a paper, do your online assignments for the week, and also research some information for an upcoming presentation. The best thing to do is to set aside all but one task. So, for this example, you want to give all your attention to writing your paper. That means turning off the TV, cell phones, social media pings, closing your door, and putting all your attention on writing.

- By giving all your attention to the task without distraction, you can get your current task done much more quickly and with fewer mistakes. Your work will be of higher quality as well. Another benefit to being focused is that your creativity will kick in too. You'll come up with new ideas associated with the task at hand.

- Being connected online and having lots of other distractions that take away your focus can affect your stress levels as well as your productivity. When you aren't focused, you don't get as much done as you could if you were truly focused on the task you're doing.

- Focusing on one thing for a certain period of time helps you think better. Having your mind scattered over several tasks at once keeps you from thinking about what you are actually doing. You only have time to complete a task quickly before you must move on to the next one. All the while, you are trying to remember everything that has to be done. When you focus, you are able to think about only one thing for that period of time.

- Focusing allows your subconscious to do the work. Think about when you learned to ride a bike or drive a car. It was difficult in the beginning, but when you began focusing on what you were doing, your subconscious took over and helped you learn. The same is true in your everyday tasks in college. Once you begin focusing solely on one task, your subconscious helps you do them quicker and easier.

It's important for you to focus on one task at a time to become more productive, do better quality work, and be less stressed. Focusing can help you be more creative and have more happiness.

Multitasking is overrated

If you're like most people, you spend your day multitasking. You're probably so used to multitasking that you don't even realize when you're doing it. After all, it's a skill many students live by. Many students believe multitasking saves them time. There are many reasons why multitasking is bad. It's better to focus instead, though. Focusing lets you concentrate on one task or thought at a time, helping you create a better result for each task.

Many people like to multitask because they become bored working on one task at a time. So, if everybody is multitasking, why can it be so bad?

The simple answer is that we do not actually multitask; we actually task switch. Your brain has to switch from one task to the next task. This switching takes time for your mind to change into the right mindset for the new task. Plus, each time you switch, you have to take the time to remember where you left off.

1. Multitasking leads to attention and memory loss. According to a study by Harvard Professor Clifford Nass, in findings published in the Proceedings of the National Academy of Science, people who use online social media and other forms of electronic communications have trouble focusing their attention and have lower scores on memory tests.

2. Cognitive performance is actually diminished. A recent study by Zheng Wang, a professor at Ohio State University, showed that multitasking caused students to feel more productive, but revealed the students were actually reducing their cognitive skills abilities such as studying.

3. It really turns people off when you are interacting with them. People who multitask often find themselves coming in direct contact with others. If you only half pay attention to others, answering texts and phone calls while talking to them, you will quickly lose their respect.

4. Multitaskers often lose productivity. Switching between tasks is counter-productive. You lose time and concentration every time you switch to a different task.

5. Multitaskers are less likely to finish one quality project. They may finish all their tasks for the day, but they will most likely be sub-par than if they had focused solely on one to completion.

Multitasking makes it difficult to focus entirely on each task you are doing. You are thinking about emails you have to respond to when writing a report and the phone calls you need to return even while you are thinking about the next task on your to-do list. This type of working environment doesn't do anything but cause you stress. Instead of multitasking among several tasks, you should prioritize your tasks and break them up into workable time chunks.

Tips To Improve Focus

Maybe you want to focus on a single task but find yourself easily distracted. You find it difficult to focus on what you are doing because you find your mind wandering, you're worrying about everything, or maybe you just have way too many things you need to do to make a choice of just one task to start with. Here are some valuable tips on how to improve focus.

Meditate

Try to allocate at least 20 minutes each day to meditate. If you can't dedicate that much time, you can still do a short breathing exercise. Focus on your breathing, really focusing on the air, how it touches your nostrils and enters your lips. How does it feel as it escapes? Your mind may wander, filling with thoughts. When this happens, bring your thoughts back to focusing on your breathing. Continue this process for several minutes. Regulating your breathing relaxes your circulatory system and brings you a sense of peace.

Listen

Listen to music to help improve your focus. Really concentrate on the music. Try to focus on a single instrument.

Cut goals into small targets

Having an end goal in mind while working on the tasks to achieve it can frustrate you because your target goal might be too big or difficult. Your results won't be quick, and it may seem like you aren't getting any closer to the end. Instead of working toward the ultimate end goal, break it down into smaller, more achievable goals you can reach within a few days. Then cross each smaller goal off your list as you achieve it.

Time clock

Work within your body's most comfortable time period. Maybe you work best early in the morning before sunrise. Or late at night. Work when you are most productive. For example, many authors get up early to do their writing, while artists often do their best work late at night.

Light meals

Have you ever eaten a big meal for lunch only to feel lethargic and weighed down all afternoon? Eating a heavy meal slows you down and makes you sleepy. If you eat light meals on a regular basis, it will keep you alert and help keep your body in good mental and physical condition.

Exercise

Exercise your mind and body every day. Do crossword puzzles. Engage in lively discussions. Build something that's creative. A simple 30-minute walk every day goes a long way to keep your body healthy.

Force yourself

You may need to push yourself some when you're feeling lazy. If you are hitting a mental roadblock, though, take some time away from the task. Do something else until you can regain your focus on the original task.

Learning to improve your focus will take time, but it is worth it. Begin by implementing one or two of these tips into your day to begin changing how well you can become focused.

Strategies To Improve Focus

You'd be surprised by how many people lose track of where their time goes. They might think they are focused on a single task but are they really? One way to find out is to keep track of how you spend your time for a week. You might find out you've been wasting time on little things like checking Instagram or TikTok once an hour.

Here are my strategies for improving your focus and increasing your productivity:

Track your time. Analyze the results after a week. Tweak and get rid of time wasters.

Plan your week. At the end of your week, find a quiet spot to plan out your week's tasks. Write down key assignments and schedule them into your planner. Don't forget to add in social activities that you participate in as well.

Prioritize your list. Break down your tasks from most important to least important. Use a calendar to mark out blocks of uninterrupted time (anywhere from 15 to 60 minutes) to work on each one.

Eliminate what isn't essential. It is often difficult for students to outsource activities, but if you have a crazy week coming up, maybe your roommate or a friend can do the shopping, cleaning, and laundry this week while you take over things the following week.

Set your goals. Break down big or long-term goals into smaller weekly or daily goals to make them easier to focus on.

Set aside a specific amount of time. Each day set aside a specific time for checking/answering email and social media. It could be the first thirty minute task of the day, lunch, or maybe the ten minutes before your next class. Don't be stopping in the middle of a task to check your email. The same goes for social media channels as well.

Do away with multitasking. It takes a while to learn how to focus on one project at a time but stick with it, and it will become a habit. Finish one project/task before moving on to the next one. Become laser-focused on one task at a time. This can really increase your productivity.

Make a distraction to-do list. The Internet has made it easy for us to become quickly distracted. As soon as we want to look something up, we hop on the Internet to do a search. "I wonder what's happening on Facebook." "What was the name of the actor in that movie?" "How long will it take me to drive to the beach tomorrow?" Anytime we get distracted like this, it takes about 25 minutes to get back to the original task. So instead, next time you want to look up something or an idea pops in your head, jot it down on a piece of paper (or, even better, use Evernote).

Learn to say NO. If you already have a full day's task list, don't feel like you have to take on another project for someone else.

Create an environment that works for you. Do you need a quiet space, free from people, phones, and television noise? Ideally, you would set up your own private space. Decorate it in soothing colors, inspiring artwork, and a comfortable chair. The reality is that the best most students can do to find a quiet spot in the campus library.

If you focus better while listening to music or some kind of ambient noise, be sure to have a good headset to make that happen.

Take a break when needed. Short breaks help break up boredom and burnout when you're working on a big project. Get up and walk around the room. Do some yoga stretches.

Use an app. Downloading an app on your phone can boost your productivity and concentration. Apps like Evernote can keep you organized and keep track of distractions. An app like Brainwave can be downloaded to your iPhone. In this app, you can choose settings like Concentration Boost and Problem Solving, Brainstorming, or Memory Boost and Creative Thinking. There are other apps that help you stay focused and productive, as well.

The strategies for becoming more focused are extensive. Make lists. Remove distractions. Set up your ideal environment. You need to find what works best for your style of working.

Exercises to Improve Focus

When TV newscaster Diane Sawyer was asked the secret to her success, she said, "I think the one lesson I've learned is there is no substitute for paying attention."

Did you know improving your focus can be done with different types of simple exercises? It's true. Something as simple as getting exercise on a daily basis can improve your brain function, which leads to better focus. Most of the time, focus exercises take less than ten minutes to do. Check out these to get you started:

- Mutter to yourself. It might seem like you're crazy, but talking to yourself either out loud or not, helps you pay attention, calms you emotionally, and tells you to act.

- Trade your caffeine for cardio. Caffeine gives you a boost, which makes it easier to concentrate. But you might find it harder to focus when you're not buzzed. A better way to keep your mind stimulated is with physical exercise. Exercise triggers the release of chemicals in the brain that affect our learning and memory, which in the end, are what help us focus.

- Drink more water. Mild dehydration can lead to distraction. Being even as little as two percent dehydrated can affect your ability to concentrate on cognitive activities.

- Get plenty of sleep. Getting at least seven hours of good quality sleep each night helps your body and mind rejuvenate and leads to better concentration and focus during the day.

How to deal with focus issues

You probably already know how hard it is to focus on something. Focus issues are often the result of different things like boredom, lack of interest, or even fatigue. Concentration can often be attributed to how motivated and interested we are in the task. There are ways to deal with focus issues.

Supplements can help you when you are having focus issues. Vitamins like the B complex group, Biotin or vitamin H, and lecithin all help improve your memory. Eating the right foods can help you better focus as well since you will be getting the supplements from the foods to help with brain-healthy foods like lean meat, beans, oranges, peanut butter, and oysters.

Consult with your physician if you find you can't focus on any one thing for any length of time. Lack of focus can be a symptom of several different conditions, including depression. Get a thorough checkup to rule out any physical causes of your lack of focus issues.

When working on projects on your computer and online, make sure you only have tabs open that are relevant to what you are doing. This keeps you from getting distracted by all that fun information floating around the Internet.

Make your tasks routine. Set up a routine for tasks that you do every day. For example, check your email and social media at the same time every day. Just like you probably have a routine when you wake up, you should also have a routine when working.

Separate your day into a time for creating, time for your classes and schoolwork, communication, and time for yourself. Split the day up in whatever way works best for you.

Dealing with focus issues causes your productivity to drop. By learning how to take care of your focus issues through your diet, exercise, and routines, you can be more productive.

Applied Focus

You can increase your productivity and accomplish more in less time by using a technique called applied focus. Applied focus can help you avoid the little distractions that will often derail your efforts at productivity.

How applied focus increases productivity

Applied focus is similar to the Pomodoro Technique, but the sessions are longer. Applied focus is a strategy that helps you multiply your productivity. Each session is 45-minutes long, with a 15-minute shift in focus. Or you can do 90-minutes, followed by a 30-minute shift in focus. In other words, you stop focusing intentionally on your task and do something completely different in the shift focus period.

During the focused session, though, you don't allow anything to distract you (except a dire emergency). Phone calls are out, email is off, texting and Facebook are off-limits.

Here are some guidelines (be sure to adjust them as necessary to fit your individual situation):

- Open only one browser or application window at a time. So if you're writing a paper, only have Word, Google Docs, or text pad open.

- Keep your sessions timed. Don't go past your planned 45 or 90 minute session. No matter how focused you are, you need a break.

- Get away from your task. Get up from your desk, walk around, get a drink or snack. Give your mind a break.

- Be prepared ahead of time. Do your research during a different applied focus session than from the writing session. That way, you're able to concentrate on the writing alone.

- Have a session set up for email, telephone, and social media time.

Applied focus sessions can increase your productivity, but it will take some getting used to. Start slowly by scheduling one or two sessions a day. Once you become used to the routine, you will notice an improvement in your concentration and productivity.

How A Brain Dump Can Help You Focus

Have you heard of "brain dump"? It's a very effective exercise to help you clear your mind and allows you to focus on tasks at a time. The big problem a brain dump addresses are the fact that we all have constant thoughts, ideas, questions, and concerns running through our brain. A brain dump allows you to consciously address them, get them on paper, and thus keep them from distracting you later on.

Here's what you need to do a brain dump. Get a notebook, a pen, and set aside a little quiet time to do this. If you're more comfortable typing, open a word document or the likes. That being said, there is some real value in going the old-fashioned way of pen and paper.

Start writing everything that comes to mind. Don't judge, don't edit, and don't skip over anything. Any ideas for projects, to-dos, and the likes go in the notebook. Don't try to sort or organize them. Just let them flow from your brain to the paper. Of course, you don't have to write down random thoughts. The idea is to get all those project ideas, things you want to for your school work, new strategies you want to try at work, or even that idea you had for a trip. Order and topic don't matter. The fact that you want to start jogging again can go right next to that list of potential new ideas you want to type up.

Take your time, don't force it, and take a breather every now and again. This exercise can be quite exhausting, but it is incredibly helpful and freeing. Think of it as a reboot for your brain that dumps all the RAM memory. It frees up a lot of space and helps you focus on the tasks that are truly important without being distracted by random thoughts.

What you do with your brain dump is up to you. You can simply tear out the pages and stick them in a drawer. There's value in the simple act of dumping them out of your brain.

You can also go through your brain dump pages a few days later and make lists of what you want to do and focus on. For example, you may make a list of good study-related ideas that you should try to implement over the coming weeks. You may also decide to cross out and disregard a lot of what you've written down, and that's ok too. Another list could capture any school improvement type projects you thought of that are worth pursuing.

Going through your brain dump like this allows you to sort and categorize the information into a format that you can work with, one task at a time. This is much more productive than having those random thoughts running through your head, taking up valuable brain space. I hope you give this brain dump technique a try. Don't just do it once and be done. Do brain dumps as needed to help you stay focused and productive.

The 5-Second Rule

As discussed earlier, sticking to the "5-second rule" can help you tremendously when it comes to ending procrastination and improving productivity. As a reminder, waiting for more than five seconds to do something makes it much harder to do it.

When it comes to learning how to say "no," you have to ditch any worries or concerns about what the other person will say or feel about you and just do it. You owe it to yourself to get things done for yourself before you tackle projects and favors for other people. So, when it comes to saying "no," just do it, and do it within the first five seconds of the request.

Be a Velvet-Covered Brick

Being a velvet-covered brick means having a hard-stance on the inside while being soft on the outside. Simply put, being a velvet-covered brick allows you to tell people very hard things in ways that minimize the possibility of hurting people's feelings.

For example, if another student asks you to help him out with a report that he needs to submit within an hour, but you have your own projects to finish as well, rather than bluntly saying, "No! I have my own things to finish." You could say something like, "I'm really sorry, but I also have to finish a report for that same class. As much as I would love to help you, I'm afraid that it would put me behind. I'm really sorry, but I'll have to say no this time."

By gently telling your friend no, you make them understand that you have your own work to do but that you still value them and might be able to help them in the future. However, you need to remember that a gentle tone of voice can make the hardest responses gentle as well.

What's next?

Learning how to focus on one task at a time takes time and commitment. In our busy lives, we are pulled in many directions at one time. It's best to begin your journey on a more focused life gradually by implementing the tips and strategies I have outlined.

Focus is such an important part of how productive you are. If you can focus on one task for a set amount of time, you will be more productive in a shorter amount of time than you have been. Putting aside your tendency to multitask will improve your productivity as well since you will be able to finish one task before you move on.

Removing distractions can help you focus as well. Create an environment that you feel comfortable in and that fits with how you work. If you're a morning person, then focus on your important assignments and vice versa for night owls.

Eat healthy and nutritious foods to keep your brain strong and able to concentrate. Exercise daily, meditate daily, and take time to enjoy nature and your family.

Now that you have a handful of strategies for improving your productivity, it's time to put them into action and incorporate them into your daily routine. Remember that productivity waxes and wanes due to a variety of different factors. It's important to run with any bursts of motivation that you have and impart some of these tools when you find that your productivity is lacking.

Whatever you decide to do with your life, you need to make sure you fill it with passion, enthusiasm and be in line with the values you have in mind. This is the real secret to increasing your productivity so that you can get more done in less time.

Improved productivity isn't something that will come to you overnight, but rather something that you have to consciously work at every day. It will take your time and work to develop the right habits that will allow you to improve your productivity. However, with enough practice and persistence, you can improve your productivity so that you can finally get more done in less time.

Chapter 8:
Peak Performance Secrets - What Separates Super Performers from Everybody Else

"Peak Performance in life isn't about succeeding all the time or even being happy all the time. It's often about compensating, adjusting, and doing the best you can with what you have right now." - *Ken Ravizza*

Pikes Peak

Pike's Peak is a mountain that rises over 8,000 feet. This particular mountain has a paved road that is used for a variety of racing, from sports cars to marathoners. Its roadway is approximately 13.5 miles long and is considered to be one of the hardest ½ marathon roads in the world.

Most people cannot fathom running a marathon, much less one that has such an incline. This makes it a perfect opportunity to showcase peak performance.

Peter Strudwick was born without feet and deformities in both his arms. When he was born, it was a time when doctors and some parents would not allow a child to live, as they felt that nothing would ever be accomplished by the child. Many people of the time felt that such children would place too large a burden on parents and should not be allowed to enter the world. Peter's mother was not one of those parents, and she left Europe to bring her child to the United States.

I could discuss Peter in a lengthy novel, but to illustrate his ability to get peak performance out of his mind and body, we will cut to the chase. Peter ran Pike's Peak 4 times. He had to develop a special way of balancing as he had no feet, and his legs ended in stumps. Peter was able to coach his body to respond to the signals his brain sent out and get himself to excel. His ability was so great that when he got a rock in his running shoe, he continued to run and relabel what the pain meant to him. Instead of telling himself how much it hurt, he coached his mind to believe he was loving the experience.

Many people believe that you must rely on your inner talent in order to achieve peak performance. Talent is only a small part. In some cases, those with a limited talent for their chosen profession succeed anyway. They succeed by using elements like grit, deliberate practice, and perseverance.

When you decide that peak performance in all areas of your life will enhance and enrich your life, there are several steps to work on. Start with your "big" why and then ask yourself, "How will I stay motivated each day?" Move on to developing your grit, your ability to push through no matter what. Can you see, feel, and taste what your peak performance will look like? If not, learn the techniques of visualization, mental rehearsal, and practice, practice, practice.

Now that you are super excited and clearly ready to jump into peak performance, I will highlight the 21 key traits and habits of peak performers. By the end of this chapter, you will have a clear roadmap of the journey ahead of you. Make this a fun journey. Enjoy the ride and then the outcome.

21 Traits and Habits of Peak Performers

Here are the habits and skills that you should work on to become a top performer. By adopting the mindset, traits, and habits of a peak performer, you can transform your life. It just takes a plan and massive action with intent. Think and act like a champion!

1) Passion

It is passion that allows champion athletes and peak performers to perform to the best of their abilities no matter what happens in life. One of the most passionate baseball players was Pete Rose. Sliding into base, feet first takes drive and grit, but Pete took it a step further. Pete really did risk serious injury by going headfirst with his arms outstretched to quickly tag the base. The potential for injury more than doubled when he adopted this approach. He was so passionate about the game that he would do something other pro baseball players of his time would not. Pete's work ethic earned him the nickname "Charlie Hustle," but unfortunately for Pete, his gambling habit got him banned from the sport he loved so much.

Passion goes hand in hand with pain and pleasure. It has been shown that people will do anything to avoid pain and will seek pleasure instead. While some peak performers may do things that seem painful to others, the peak performer has found huge reasons why they seek to do the things they do.

For example, we could look at professional wrestlers. While their moves are scripted, they still suffer pain every night that they perform. The peak performers from this group find that at the end of their career, they are so mangled from years of taking falls and hard bumps. With that happening, they cannot walk properly and are in constant pain. So, one would ask, if they know at the start of their careers that this is what the end will look like, why would they do it? The answer to that is passion. They are passionate about hearing the roar of the crowd and seeing the crowd react to what they do.

It is passion that drives singers to perform night after night for sometimes up to a year. Passion also drives businesspeople not only to succeed in life but to contribute as much as possible to the underprivileged.

In the business world, the Rockefeller name is well known. Laurance S. Rockefeller believed that being alive meant being able to give, and he had several foundations set up to do just that. When peak performers put everything they have into their careers, whether it is professional sports or business, it is the passion that drives them to seek more pleasure from what they do.

Action Steps:

A) Make a list of what your interests are. Beside each one, write out why you want to do this. Then narrow it down to the top three, using the biggest Why's.

B) Discover what your talent is. How does it excite you? Is it something you would do for free 24/7?

C) Even if you would do it for free 24/7, don't let it consume you. Instead, integrate it into your life. It is now a part of your life, without overwhelming your thinking.

2) Drive and Motivation

Understanding that taking a particular action will result in reaching the top is what many peak performers use to motivate themselves. We can start by using Tony Robbins as a prime example. Early in his career, Tony and his team booked themselves as speakers.

The people on Tony's team would book between 3-5 talks per week. Tony wanted to be the best and give a peak performance every time he spoke. He used the end goal as a motivation tool to book as many as three talks per day, at least five days a week. His two goals were to perfect his performance and gain the knowledge he needed by working ten times harder than anyone else around him. Tony and other peak performers have what is called "drive." It is a dynamic quality that allows a peak performer to wake up two to four hours earlier than the normal person and get a jump on the day.

Ryan Seacrest is known as one of the hardest working people in Hollywood. He wasn't the smartest in school or even the best athlete, but he excelled in driving himself to succeed. After his school day had ended, Ryan went to the radio station and worked as an intern until midnight. Honing his craft this way and being driven, he now hosts more than one television show at a time. Growing up, he was overweight. Ryan uses his drive and motivation to schedule his workouts, just like business appointments. To pump up his game even more, he sometimes goes for a run just before the start of his hosting duties on American Idol.

Other peak performers may use the early hours to do one of several things that assist and motivate them. For example, they may get up at 4:00 am to exercise vigorously and then eat a healthy breakfast that fuels them for the first part of the day. Others may be driven to use that early time to meditate, read motivational books, or watch motivational videos. They understand the value of getting into the right state and engaging their drive factor.

Each peak performer is truly different. The key thing with peak performers is that they have discovered what works the best for them, and they do not allow others to tell them how it should be done.

Action Steps:

A) Check your positivity frequently throughout the day. Where are you on a scale of 1 to 5? If you do this and notice you are slipping from 5 down to 2, take positive action to course correct.

B) Give yourself small rewards, daily, weekly, monthly, for the work you do to stay totally motivated. Having drive and motivation should be fun, not a serious chore.

C) Have a coach or trusted friend kick your butt if you fall off the motivation bandwagon. This can also help with maintaining a positive attitude.

3) Goal Setting

Studies have shown that even people who have not hit their peak performance levels do so after learning how to write effective goals, and an action plan, with a commitment to follow through.

There is more to setting goals than just writing down, "I want to this, or I will achieve that by such and such a date." Using a special system of goal setting, like setting S.M.A.R.T. goals, puts you ahead of the average person. SMART is an acronym that you can use to guide your goal setting.

To make sure your goals are clear and reachable, each one should be:

- Specific (simple, sensible, significant).

- **M**easurable (meaningful, motivating).

- **Attainable** (agreed, achievable).

- **R**elevant (reasonable, realistic, and resourced, results-based).

- **T**ime-bound (time-based, time-limited, time/cost limited, timely, time-sensitive).

Peak performers take it a few steps further before they even sit down to write their goals. They decide first of all what their ultimate purpose in life is and how their goals can serve others like their family or specialized charities, for instance.

Writing out their core values first helps with their relationships and understanding the value of giving. Putting it down on paper helps to shift through what is really true for them or what may have been a false core value.

Peak performers look at their:

- Relationships

- Community Service and giving to others

- Health

- Creativity

- Knowledge

- Love of themselves and those who matter. Remember, you must love yourself before you can truly love others.

Once they get it down on paper, peak performers take the time to visualize each aspect and acknowledge how it makes them feel. This is how they decide if their values are true. Peak performers understand the value of combining goal setting with visualization.

While a goal may look great on paper, it really doesn't get wings until it becomes so inviting that you can see it, mentally touch and taste it.

Champions in the competitive sport arena use goal setting to improve performance in achievable bites. Their goals will, of course, be different than those of a student. The goals will include physical achievements and mental clarity, such as visualizing a certain number of times that the ball goes through the hoop without effort.

The champion athlete might have a series of goals that lead up to winning a championship ring or trophy. Each component is visualized, so when faced with the opportunity to achieve their goals, they have been there many times before in their mind. By doing this, they have already won that championship ring. Think about how powerful it is to visualize winning the cup or championship ring before you even start the season. By continuing through the season and layering the visualization and goals, the cup is already won. As a student, you can visualize a successful presentation, earning that "A," and walking across the stage at graduation.

For peak performers, goal setting is a stacking of positive actions. Goal setting helps them with the motivation we already talked about and includes gaining confidence in the abilities to set and reach targets. A peak performer in the sales area uses concise, well thought out goals to help motivate them to make the calls and contacts needed to achieve the salary they want and the bonuses that come with that.

Action Steps:

A) Believe with all your heart that goal-setting works. If you don't believe it, you will not follow through.

B) Find examples of goal setters. Who are your hero's, and do they set goals? Write down what they do to succeed.

C) Set S.M.A.R.T. goals that are performance-driven.

4) Time Management

One thing that really sets peak performers high above the crowd is an understanding that "it is up to them." They know that they are 100% responsible for managing their time and going into peak performance mode. By the time they do look to a coach for assistance in fine-tuning their ability to perform, they are already way ahead of the pack.

For peak performers, time management is less about the actual time put into a task and more about eliminating time stealers. They learn to discover the most important tasks, which they must focus on, and how to delete unnecessary tasks.

Peak performers have their time mapped out. They know how much time they will spend on exercise, research, actual work, leisure, and all the other components. Their days are not filled with, "okay, finished with that, what should I do next?" What really sets them above the crowd is the ability to look at what is working and what is not. They can quickly change their focus to a different path that will bring them the success they desire.

Peak performers do not get wrapped up in perceived failure but forge ahead with drive in order to make the adjustment to their plan work. At the beginning of their goal setting and time management, they already understand that a quick but effective adaption to what the day has sprung upon them will likely become necessary.

Peak performers map out their goals long term. They understand that the goal may be altered by the time they begin to work on it, but they have it written down. In an interview, a peak performer would have no hesitation answering the question, "Where do you see yourself in 5 years? What about 10 years?" They have a firm image planted in their mind's eye.

Action Steps:

   A. Figure out how long each task related to performance takes.

   B. Stay away from time stealers. Move with deliberate action.

   C. Don't bite off too big a chunk. Set manageable, attainable
       goals.

5) Discipline

Without discipline, there is no peak performance. Slacking off or not giving 100% focus means that the outcome will not be worthy of peak performance. The truly disciplined peak performer does not allow distractions to get in the way. They may wake up in the morning and find they are unmotivated but will quickly find a way to snap to attention and get in the target seeking mode.

Peak performers learn to remove distractions from their lives. They understand that once a distraction is gone, it makes the road to peak performance easier. A master of self-discipline can remove anything, from food to tech toys, in order to make the road smoother.

Action Steps:

   A. You need to be 100% clear on what you want.

   B. What is causing you pain? We will do anything to move out
       of pain, so write down the painful parts of why you are not
       practicing self-discipline and learn to change them to
       pleasure.

   C. Set goals that require effort and reward that effort.

6) Grit

A person may be exceptionally talented but fail to do as well as others due to a lack of grit. When a person is able to mix together passion and perseverance, they have the formula for grit. A talented, world-class runner may suffer a physical or even emotional injury and fail to deliver during the big race. The runner with true grit will push aside the issue and continue to run at a top-level. A person may not have grit, but when they want to be a peak performer, they can develop it. There is even a test available where they can check the level of grit they have and then make an action plan to take it to the next level.

Check it out here: https://angeladuckworth.com/grit-scale/

The person who developed the grit scale is Angela Duckworth. She has been studying grit for many years and is the leading expert. What studies have found is that grit outweighs a person's intelligence and talent. Talent is wonderful, but if a person hits an obstacle and backs off frequently, then peak performance is out of the question.

A person lucky enough to have parents that were gritty, will in most cases, be the same way when they grow up. If the parents worked hard and put everything into their jobs and raising children, this is usually passed on. Not everyone is that lucky, and they may need to develop grit on their own.

Focusing on your course work and one or two campus organizations is a good place to start. Rather than giving up when you have a bad day, test result, or grade, students with grit just buckle down and find out how to course correct.

To be gritty, figure out what you are passionate about. Next up, be clear about what your goals are short term and long term, writing down why you won't stop until you achieve them. Grit means knocking down the walls that get thrown up in your pathway. Grit means not kicking yourself in the butt if you fail.

It means picking yourself up off the ground and getting right back at it. When things go wrong, people with grit see an opportunity. Many of the products that are on the market today come from failure that someone with grit turned into a new opportunity.

Being gritty means you will excel. Your belief system should scream, "I will never give up." Just listen to Winston Churchill's famous speech. It contains all the right words to define how gritty the British would be during World War II. To make it easier, find and surround yourself with people who are already gritty and feed off of each other.

Action Steps:

A) When grit is a word that is not in your vocabulary, pick one area of your life to develop grit. Complete that and then pick another area.

B) You develop the grit by getting a win, rejoice in that win and then layer on another win.

7) Perseverance

Building perseverance is something that all champions and peak performers work on daily, and you should as well. The rule of thumb is to strive to be 1% better each day, or each week, or even each month on a task or performance that you need to excel at. As adults, we sometimes lose the perseverance attitude. Think about small children and all the things they had to keep repeating until they are finally "a big kid now." Walking, tying your shoes, and riding a bike comes with perseverance.

Champion basketball players may pick one aspect of the game that they know they can improve on. It may be shooting foul shots as an example. They build perseverance and focus by taking the time each day to be 1% better at sinking the basketball repeatedly without hitting the rim. They tell themselves nothing is sweeter than "all net."

In business, a person may choose to build perseverance in making the sale. They work out what they need to improve on to close the deal and practice that each and every day. As a student, striving to improve your Grade Point Average (GPA) each semester is a great target.

Action Steps:

A) Set a major goal. Figure out what will stand in your way and decide ahead of time how to break down that brick wall.

B) Understand there is no failure, only learning. Know when it is time to stop and re-exam your goal, instead of ripping yourself apart for not achieving. Did you have the right, WHY?

C) Feedback from coaches is great; however, you need to learn to do self-feedback as well. Learn how to ask the right questions about your performance and what needs to be tweaked.

8) Focus

Focus is not a simple task. Many people want to try and multi-task, and that leads to confusion and uncompleted projects. While it is advised that peak performers stay off the smartphone, it is actually best to put it in another room to avoid temptation.

Setting up blocks on social media sites keeps the peak performer from getting distracted. To be a peak performer, you need a focus that is laser-sharp. Think of a magnifying glass with the sun beaming down. That narrowed glass area of focus will lead to wood sparking into flames.

A number of people may believe that to focus, one should just eliminate distraction and then get down to the job at hand. Peak performers may intuitively understand that it is much more than that. There are internal blocks that need to be broken down and eliminated, which will allow the person to truly develop a laser focus on performance. There are three types of focus that peak performers must be aware of.

First and foremost, is the inner focus of what is going on in our heads at any particular time? After that, we look at outer focus; what outer obstacles or opponents stand in our way? True leaders already know and understand the third focus, which is empathy focus for the team or partners. They understand they have to have a focus on building them up to be the best they can be. For a peak performer, it is essential to understand which focus is the current focus that is required.

For students, maintaining focus can be very difficult. Championship athletes have found a way to cope with this. They are able to slip into a state of complete relaxation, no matter what is going on around them.

Basketball great Michael Jordan was a true champion with this focus technique. When the heat of the game was overwhelming, and it was break time, Jordan could mentally trigger himself into a state of complete calm. When the camera panned the bench, Jordan would appear as if he was sitting on the beach, listening to the wave's crash on the shore.

These two to three moments of absolute calmness would allow him to reset his focus for playing at the very top of his game. For all peak performers, it is necessary not to overwhelm your senses by focusing too long and too hard on any given project. Taking a moment and then resetting your focus will give you the best results.

Action Steps:

A) Work on getting deep, restful sleep. It is essential to maintaining focus throughout the day.

B) You need to eliminate distractions…from people, social media, and other distractions.

C) Commit to practicing your focus. When you lose focus, do ten pushups, lose focus again, do fifteen, and so on.

9) Practice. Practice. Practice

How can champion chess players move their pieces so quickly? It comes from practice, practice, and more practice. Over years of practice, their brain is able to quickly calculate what the opponent will do and how many moves are required to avoid capture, as an example.

In the game of cribbage, the hands are counted mainly in groups of what cards add up to fifteen. A champion cribbage player does not need to count his hand as a beginner does. They have held the same hand multiple times in their years of play/practice and instinctively can say what the total of points are they have accumulated.

Studies conducted state that we need approximately 10,000 hours of consistent practice to finally become an expert in any area. Tony Robbins, a motivational speaker of note, believes there is a short cut, and he calls it modeling. He finds an expert and basically copies everything the expert does, including that person's belief systems.

Peak athletes use practice with performance goals to hit their best efforts. A champion golfer may write down that they will continue to practice until they can sink a putt from a certain distance ten times in a row. At the point in time that they hit the performance goal, they reward themselves for a job well done.

Basketball player LeBron James takes practice very seriously. In practice, he will work on each possible type of shot that he may be called on to make in a crucial game. LeBron gets his teammates to assist by setting up game scenarios with limited time on the clock. When watching a basketball game, people may look at an extremely difficult situation, and then the shot that LeBron James just made, wondering how he possibly could do that? The truth is, he has already done such a thing in his daily practice many times over.

Action Steps:

A. Focus on practice only. Don't try to multi-task, like doing practice, while texting or talking to others.

B. Break your practice into small manageable chunks.

C. Have a practice schedule. Get rid of distractions.

10) Work on Your Strengths (Not Your Weaknesses)

Studies done by social psychologists have shown that working on and honing your strengths has many benefits. Performance and productivity skyrocket, and this, in part, can be attributed to the confidence and satisfaction that people feel.

Working on weaknesses may cause a feeling of inadequacy or other negative emotions. By doing studies on improving strengths, the psychologists also found that when the strengths were at the very peak, the weaknesses held no weight and were irrelevant. Your weakness must be brought up to an average level, but beyond that average level, studies show it is much more effective to lean into your strength rather than spend a bunch of time trying to improve your weakness.

Peak performers work on their strengths and understand that doing so gives them energy bursts to carry on and not lose focus. Knowing they have a strength already and are working diligently to improve it gives the champion or peak performer a sense of happiness. All the focus is on the positive strength and making it even stronger.

In championship hockey, the peak performer understands that the more shots they take, the more goals they score. By focusing on making sure to get into the right position to receive the puck at all times, they build up the strength of getting the shot off as quickly as possible and then look to repeat the process immediately if a goal is not scored.

The great Wayne Gretzky told everyone why he was such a prolific goal scorer. "I go to where the puck will be, not where it currently is." He had such mental strength that he could override the desire to chase the puck but instead, always go to the spot where he knew it will eventually come to.

Action Steps:

    A. Do you know what your strengths are? You need to be aware before you can build them up to the highest level.

    B. Discover the different ways you can use your strengths in all areas of your life.

    C. Work on different methods to make your strengths as strong as possible.

11) Get Into the Flow

Getting into flow has been studied and found to be essential for any peak performance. There are two elements of flow, called the ideal performance state and the zone of optimal functioning. When in the flow, peak performers will lose track of time as they are internalizing calmness, focus, and total relaxation in spite of outside pressure.

Peak performers have a number of methods of getting into the flow and accelerating their performance smoothly and efficiently. They start by committing to taking responsibility for everything that happens in their lives. They believe that what happens to them occurred from their thoughts and their actions. Because they take 100% responsibility, they are able to change what is happening by shifting thoughts and actions. When they have a limiting belief, they know they are responsible, and they work to change their beliefs so that the belief serves them.

With internal beliefs aligned, peak performers look to their verbal language to ensure they are not using words that limit them, such as, "I hope, or I wish." They are masters of how they speak internally and externally.

In order not to interrupt the flow, peak performers never agree to do things that they are not fully on board with. Of course, in college, we are stuck doing a bunch of things we may not be on board with! That's just part of the life of a student. But students have a habit of getting involved in a lot of optional stuff. When suggestions are made that will disrupt their flow, peak performers always need to be able to say, "Yes, that is a great idea, I can commit to that." When there is a hesitating moment, the peak performer knows this is not right for them, and they will walk away.

Joy and passion are what peak performers seek to enhance. They will flow smoothly through the day because they do not look back and wonder if this is for them and did, they do the right thing or choose the right next action. They ride life as if it is a smooth-flowing river without angry rapids. College is hard, but if you stay focused on the end game, you can actually find yourself in a flow state more than you would have ever imagined.

Action Steps:

A. Everything is a choice. Your choice. If you are not happy with your performance in college, the flow will be very difficult. Love the experience and work you do, and flow will follow as you are engrossed in what you do.

B. Making sure your brain is on laser focus mode is crucial. Get rid of the mental garbage flowing around in your head.

C. Be your own security guard. Things and people that distract you must either go or be told to come back at a more suitable time.

12) Confidence

Can a person be confident if they failed a course, flunked an exam, bombed a test, or even changed their major? They can if they are a peak performer and have trained themselves to be confident even in the face of adversity. What do you call a baseball player that gets only three hits every ten times at the plate? Allstar! Tiger woods loses more golf tournaments than he wins, but he is still the greatest golfer of this generation and, by many accounts, of all-time.

Peak performers do not "wait" until they feel confident and then attempt to perform. They use muscle memory of the brain. There are stored memories of all the times they were confident in life, and they build on that. The so-called failures are pushed to the back of the memory vault or erased completely.

When a peak performer starts to feel a lack of confidence, analyzing the situation typically will reveal that the issue is the stress of performing. The confidence to perform is still there, but the stress is overwhelming the brain and not allowing the confidence to do its job. The remedy is to ensure that stress levels never get that high, that it can overtake the muscle memory of confidence.

The peak performer needs to understand that confidence relies on several things. As discussed, stress levels play a part, and another would be self-esteem. Millions of students have failed a class, made a bad grade, changed their major, or even transferred schools multiple times. Many were able to recover just fine, and of course, some lost their confidence. In the back of their mind, it is possible to feel "not good enough" or "will never be as good as." These mental images need to be dealt with at the early stage, and once they are, confidence in ability begins to rise, and it gets harder to knockdown. Remember, you have faced challenges and obstacles before and have overcome them.

Action Steps:

A. Dwelling in your head means that you are immersed in negativity and go back and forth, arguing positions with yourself. Negative thoughts must be dismissed and replaced with positive ones.

B. When feeling doubtful about your confidence, write down all the times you were confident and how that came to be. This reassures you that you can do it.

C. Make a workable action plan, do this, then do this. When you know where you are going, the journey is clear in your brain.

13) Be Teachable And Coachable

Peak performers "may" understand that even if they have grit, talent, and persistence for starters, they are still short one thing that they do not have within them. The best of the best still know they need a high-level coach or mentor. While they know in their heart where their ability is, they know there are small things that they are unable to see and correct. A coach is required to spot the issue, offer constructive criticism, and put together a game plan to correct the issue.

Mentors have been where you are going. They have faced the challenges you will be facing, and their experience can speed your path to success. Sometimes we can be slow to seek help and assistance. We think that we can do it all on our own and only seek help as a last resort.

Even top athletes sometimes struggle to recognize that coaches can help. In the case of mixed martial arts superstar Georges St. Pierre, his thought process had him believing that his physical abilities were more than enough. In fact, he had the negative idea that only weak-minded people needed to hire performance coaches.

After being introduced to and working with a peak performance coach, Georges went on to a 7-year reign as a world champion. He now believes that this would not have been possible without the use of a specialized coach.

As a student, you may think tutoring centers and professor office hours are for students who are struggling. Nothing is further from the case. Students in the universities' academic coaching or tutoring centers are actually the top students in their fields. They have taken the courses you are taking and likely know your professor's personal nuisances and pet peeves. They not only can help you understand difficult concepts, but they can also help guide you and direct your focus. Building relationships with your professors can help you way beyond the course work. They can help guide you toward the proper career choices, internships, and even scholarships.

Many universities have mentorship programs with alumni and leaders in the community. Mentorship and coaching are available if you seek it out. Even if your university doesn't have a mentorship program or if you aren't selected for the program, you can find your own coach/mentor. LinkedIn is a great resource to achieve this goal. Reach out to people you admire and ask if you can have 20 minutes of their time for an informational interview. Ask if they can recommend some blogs or industry resources for you to further your knowledge. Ask if you can reach back out to them in the future with additional questions should they arise. Always make sure to thank them for their time and send a thank you email. As you build relationships with your LinkedIn connections, ask a few of them if they would be comfortable mentoring you.

Action Steps:

A. Be 100% positive that coaching is right for you and that you will achieve your goals faster.

B. Do your research. Get a coach/mentor that is kick butt and positive. You want someone who will challenge you and bring out the absolute best in you.

C. Set aside time to reflect on what your coach/mentor is asking of you. It is okay to ask questions and verify what direction you are headed in.

14) Optimism and Positive Thinking

Peak performers and champions are extremely optimistic people. They can put 100% effort in every day and perhaps not see results due to factors outside their control. When they speak, they will say things like, "it didn't happen today, but it will happen tomorrow." They will repeat sayings like that for as long as it takes. In treasure hunting, Mel Fisher was a peak performer, and he repeated this saying every day for over 20 years... "today is the day." He did eventually find a massive treasure. He succeeded because he never let negative thinking take over.

Peak performers understand or learn to comprehend that mental growth is not static. Unlike people who believe that they are born with a certain amount of positive mindset and that it cannot be improved, the peak performer treats the brain like a muscle. Positive thinking or growth mindset is a practiced and acquired skill.

A peak performer will learn to focus on helping others get what they want, knowing that, in return, they will get what they need, want, and desire. When you watch a champion, you have no idea what they are saying to themselves, but if you focus closely, you will notice their body language speaks volumes. They move with confidence and make gestures that illustrate the positive state of mind they are in.

Peak performers have the growth mindset of, "I will focus on what I can control and dismiss everything else." It is the same as focusing on their strengths and not their weakness. Sure, you must pass all your classes, and you just can't disregard your weaknesses. The point is, if you are not great with numbers, you find a major that does not require a significant amount of math. Lean into your strengths and do what you need to do to bring your weaknesses up to an acceptable level.

Peak performers have learned to control their positive thinking and eliminate words or phrases that do not serve them. They never use the term, "I have to," instead they use, "I want to." This slightly different phrasing makes all the difference in the outcome of what actions they will take.

Action Steps:

A. Start and end the day with your number one positive affirmation. Say the others during the day.

B. Life throws curveballs at you all the time. Learn to take a hit and find the humor in it.

C. There will always be what people call failures. Instead, call them learning points and examine them closely to see how they can serve you.

15) Creativity (focusing on solutions, not problems)

Most people would agree that one of the best players in the NHL is Sidney Crosby. He is extremely talented and, of course, a hard worker. He is also highly creative, perhaps the most creative hockey player ever. He hates it when he misses a goal-scoring opportunity and found a creative way to deal with the issue.

He asked his teammates and coaches to help him by duplicating the exact play that he did not score on in the next day's practice. He went through the same scenario over and over until he solved the puzzle of why he did not score. Sidney Crosby believes in focusing on the solutions and does not dwell on problems.

Peak performers understand that creativity can be learned and seek out the opportunities on how to do such, as it relates to their goals. They may model those who are extremely creative and find out exactly how they think and what process they go through to come up with creative solutions.

Peak performers look for creative ways to reinvent themselves. They understand that sometimes it is necessary to "shed their skin" and come out new and improved. For example, you could look to music performers who have hit a level and aren't moving forward. They know it is time to recreate themselves.

Celine Dion can be an example as she moved from regular concerts to a full extravaganza show on stage in Las Vegas, starting in 2003. Her shows were to be so elaborate that she and her husband had a special building constructed to house her productions.

Action Steps:

A. Brainstorming is an excellent way to come up with new creative ideas. Let it flow and write it down or record it as it comes to your mind.

B. You should have journals in different areas of your life. A creativity journal works wonders for coming up with new and exciting ideas.

C. Try using "what if" as a way to come up with new ideas. For example, "what if Sasquatch is actually a version of the "Invisible Man." You cannot see him because he doesn't want you to and slips into his invisible mode. Perhaps he is actually an alien. What if... thinking sparks creativity and new ideas? This is a cartoon example, of course, but I use it to drive home the point of not self-regulating your ideas.

16) Adaptability

Peak performers really love challenges. They understand how they will grow after they meet and overcome a challenge. In their minds, it is just like being a samurai sword, which has been heated, folded, and hammered upon for 1,000's of times. In the end, the sword is unbreakable and the sharpest available.

All champions see a challenge and revel in adapting to and defeating the challenge. They recognize that success is never a straight line. They expect and anticipate setbacks.

While getting pumped to perform at their best, the peak performer avoids negative energies, such as extreme anger or getting down. They want to win badly but understand that keeping a calm head means they will avoid devastating mistakes during performance.

Action Steps:

A) Keep an open mind. As you progress through life, things can change rapidly. Don't have your feet stuck in concrete, be ready to move and roll with the punches.

B) Eliminate your "complaining button." Complaining about issues instead of being positive and flexible will keep you stuck.

C) When you can think on a grand scale, you are open to adapt to new things. Thinking small means you are stuck in neutral or even moving backward.

17) Resourcefulness

Peak performers are resourceful people. When a challenge appears before them, it means two things. First of all, they believe it will be fun to work out the puzzle, break down the walls, and crush the goals. Second, they know it means they need to put their creative thinking hat on, so they can ask themselves lots of questions and get amazing answers.

It is normal for a peak performer to ask themselves, "How would those who went before me handle this situation? What resources would they use?" As a student, you have millions who have gone before you. Often students believe their challenges are unique to them and treat every problem like they have never overcome a problem before.

Being resourceful is a matter of looking at the tools you currently have to do the job and then asking, "What other tools are available that I have not tried before, that may help me succeed." Or, "can I create a tool or system that will get the results that I want?" Your university is filled with resources to help you succeed.

Action Steps:

A. Learning is your best friend when it comes to being resourceful. The more knowledge you have, the easier it is to think outside the box and coming up with new solutions.

B. When you have ideas at your fingertips, it helps you to be resourceful when needed. Capture small ideas and write them in notes on your smartphone. When you need it flip through your phone for some ideas that you probably would not have remembered.

C. Build that persistence muscle. When you need to be resourceful, you won't give up. You will flex that muscle and find a way to get it done.

18) Personal Power Development: Working On Your Body

It's obvious that peak performers in the athletic world work on improving their body, on a consistent basis. But what about peak performers in college? To be honest, it would be almost impossible to be at a peak mental state if the physical was not taken care of.

There are many different components to get peak performance out of your body, such as proper hydration, stretching, cardio, and muscle movement.

Peak performers have a well-written plan for working on their bodies. They track progress, set goals, and make new goals once the original goals have been attained. Since technology has advanced, the peak performer will make use of tools that assist in getting the most out of their bodies. They may use a Fitbit or set up apps on their phones, which give them strenuous workouts to complete.

Peak performers are goal setters and goal achievers. When you read their goals, you will see complete sections on physical goals and mental goals. The two go hand in hand because if the body is not finely tuned, well-fueled with water and proper food, then the mind will not work properly. Loss of focus is the first thing noticed, and the ability to keep stress out of the equation is another thing that the non-physical person would see.

Action Steps:

    A. Write out an eating plan that works for you, including hydration ideas.

    B. Take your exercise routine now and bump it up. Write down how to make it better.

    C. Explore new ideas to build your cardio and your body. Make it something that will inspire you.

19) Personal Power Development: Always Learning

Feeding the mind and acquiring the knowledge you need to achieve what you want is an essential part of being a peak performer.

Peak performers love the challenge of learning new ways to reach success. They may get this from reading, listening to podcast,

YouTube videos, etc. As a student, you likely think the university is going to cover all the things you will need to know to be successful. The fact is, there likely will be a gap, and even if your university did cover everything you would need to know for your first job, how would you differentiate yourself from every other student in your major?

Head over to Indeed or LinkedIn and find six to eight jobs you would love to have upon graduation. Look at the job requirements and identify any gaps you may have, and go to work closing those gaps. For example, you are a finance major, and you learn that almost every job you would want requires a working knowledge of SQL. SQL, you think, what the heck is that? You look at your college course catalog and SQL courses are nowhere to be found. Time to go to work in the summer learning SQL on your own time, so you can land that job you really want at graduation.

Travel time is study time for the peak performer. While they may be on a five-hour flight, you will likely see them on the laptop watching a webinar or working on improving the knowledge base they already have. In the car, the peak performer listens to podcasts and believes in the idea of "the car is a university on wheels," where you fuel your mind with positive information instead of listening to the negativity produced in the media. Peak performers limit their entertainment time and lean into improving their skills.

Action Steps:

    A. Make a list of what you need to learn to differentiate yourself from other students at graduation. Example: Teach yourself to type faster or learn a computer or a foreign language.

    B. Build a library of books that relate to your future work.

    C. Decide what you are going to listen to while commuting. Motivation? Self-Development? Education?

20) Visualization

Peak performers in basketball often talk about visualizing the process for shooting a free throw from the line or driving to the basket and dunking the ball. They see each footstep they take, what the crowd sounds like, and then frame by frame as they line up, prepare, and to shoot for "nothing but net." They repeat this process over and over in their minds.

Studies have been done on the effectiveness of this mental visualization idea. A number of players actually practiced doing free throws over and over, and their improvements were recorded. Next, a similar group was asked to visualize all the steps of doing free throws. Finally, that group was taken to a basketball court where they did the free throws for real. The study showed that the visualization group improved on the free throws at the same rate as those who actually did them on the court.

A peak performer who needs to give a speech to a large group of people can prepare for the speech by doing it in visualization mode, rather than standing in the living room and giving the speech to the family.

They would do it step by step in their mind, starting with walking up to the stage and hearing the murmur of the crowd. Next, they would see themselves striding confidently across the stage and adjusting the microphone. Each step would be complete, and the ending would come with seeing the crowd on their feet, cheering and clapping.

Action Steps:

A) On a file card/post-it notes, write out the goal in big letters, and under that, write the big WHY.

B) Using file cards/post notes, write out each step that you plan to visualize. This helps to cement it in your mental images. Card one for speech-making could be getting dressed for success, card two heading to the stage, card three, walking across the stage, and so on.

C) Decide where you are going to visualize. Make sure it is a comfortable spot, with the cellphone turned off and all other distractions dealt with before you begin.

21) Images of Success: Mental self-visualization enjoying success.

For some peak performers making mental images of success comes quite easy. For others, it is a required practice and more practice. Think of images of success as physical playing cards. Try putting an image of the ace of hearts in your mind. Look at the shape of the image, the colors, and see all the details. Next, take that playing card and start moving it counterclockwise. Once you get good at pulling up the image of an ace of hearts card, you can move on to creating images of success.

Many experts recommend you create a memory storage vault for your successful images. Having a memory vault or memory library of successful images means you can pull one image out at any time during the day and view it for motivation.

The writer Stephen King explores the idea of memory vaults and even lockboxes in mind. In his sequel to The Shining, called "Dr. Sleep," the main character teaches someone how to take a horrifying ghost and put it into a small lockbox with a key. Then stashing that lockbox deep in a vault in their mind. The lockbox stays on a shelf, with the ghost trapped inside.

The success image should be one of you in moments of peak performance and show how you stand, smile, and react to success. Just imagine for a moment if you had a deck of 52 success image cards that you could display to yourself whenever you wanted. Think of how you would feel, the energy that would flow through you, and how you could use the card to move you further into massive action.

It is widely believed that the majority of top-performing athletes use a form of visualization in order to achieve peak performance. They may use mental images that they bring up into their minds, like playing cards or do full-on visualization exercises.

Visualizing success is one tool that Tom Brady has used to win multiple Super Bowls, and he is only one major success story. Basketball great Michael Jordan also used visualization to achieve records and win multiple NBA titles. Golfing great Jack Nicklaus said he never hit a shot that he did not first see in his mind.

Champion athletes often have to overcome a lot of adversity in their chosen game. While a tennis player visualizes serving aces and returning shots perfectly, athletes in combat sports and contact sports have different needs.

In combat sports, not only does the athlete visualize what they are doing but what others may do to them and how to overcome it quickly. They must master seeing themselves being hit without flinching and how to rebound. When seeing themselves knocked down and seemly unable to continue, great visualizers overcome this and see themselves rising up, shaking off the pain, and continuing onward.

Visualization can also be used as a time to reset your brain. Rapper and actor L.L. Cool J stated that he does visualization for a short time, allows himself to drift off into a type of power nap, and wake up totally refreshed, feeling like the day has just started.

The key to getting the most out of your visualization is to make it as realistic as possible. MMA champion Connor MacGregor is an expert at this. When fighting for a championship against a talented opponent, he doesn't see himself knocking out his opponent in 30 seconds. He understands there will be times in the fight when he will get in trouble. In one instance, Connor knew he would be taken to the ground. He saw himself on the ground, striking his opponents with elbows from his back and getting the better of his opponent. In case you are wondering, this is exactly what happens in the fight, and Connor maintained his title.

Challenges & Setbacks

Anything you want to achieve in life of any consequence will come with real challenges and setbacks. You must mentally prepare and visualize for those as well. My second book was not a commercial success.

My first book had become an international bestseller. Was that book just a fluke, a lucky happening? Beginners luck? After all, I thought I had done everything right. I found a great publisher and even hired a famous writing coach for a whopping $20,000. With all the pieces in place, I just knew I had a New York Times Bestseller ready to go! I was greatly disappointed with the results. But I dusted myself off, went back to work, and my third book, *"Time Management Secrets For College Students,"* was not only a huge commercial success, but it was also recently recognized as #14 on the list of 50 "Greatest College Books of All Time."

What changed from book one to book two? In book two, I lost my voice. I was not focused on making an impact and helping others, as much as I was focused on creating a huge commercial success. I listened to what the so-called experts had to say. I filtered my message to appeal to a larger audience, and in return, my true voice was lost.

The journey to success and achieving your goals is rarely a straight line. Your journey will be filled with both setbacks and positive surprises. The key to success is to stay focused on your goal, stay steadfast in your commitment, but flexible in your approach. Like Bruce Lee, maintain what is useful and discard what is not. Learn, adapt, and grow! But most importantly, stay true to yourself. If you do these things, success will take care of itself.

Action Steps:

A. Take a playing card of your choosing. Carry it with you for a few days and practice looking at it and getting that image in your mind. You should be able to see that card clearly when you pull it from memory.

B. Decide what success images will motivate you.

C. Start with one image and get it firm in your mind. Add each new image as your ability to do so increases with practice.

Six-Principle That Will Give You A Solid Foundation To Reach Your Performance Goals

Achieving Peak Performance is a continuous work in progress, and following the next six principles will give you a solid foundation to reach your performance goals much quicker while maintaining your sanity in the process.

1) Rituals

Rituals in regard to peak performance are based solely on individual needs and desires. In this section, we will look at a few things peak performers do daily to be at the top of their game.

Remember that it is okay to develop your own rituals that are specific to you. Peak performers find that starting the day off with working on their mindset is paramount. Programming the mind on a daily basis is a required ritual. There may be more than one thing that puts you in the right frame of mind to have an awesome day. Here are some of the rituals you need to consider doing on a daily basis:

- Journaling for gratitude and creativity.

- Visualization of what you want to accomplish today.

- Meditation-done outdoors in sunlight if possible.

- Working on goal setting and to-do list for the day.

- Reading mindset books and learning new skills.

- Proper exercise and nutrition to set up your day.

There may be times when you cannot do all the rituals that you have adopted for yourself each day. The key is not to get down on yourself but to look for ways to improve on what you can accomplish each day.

2) Be A Team Player and Team Builder

Peak performers understand they cannot do it by themselves, and therefore they must build the best team available. A peak performer on a sports team is a leader. They get the best out of their teammates, and the joy they feel from helping to elevate the performance of their teammates helps to raise their overall performance.

Peak performers do not belittle others. They know that they can get what they want by helping others achieve their dreams. Without an ego, they build themselves into a person that others can look up to and model for everyone to have ultimate success.

3) Assess Performance-Measure

Peak performers evaluate everything they do. There is no" winging it" in peak performance. Each time they perform either as an athlete or in their studies or careers, they assess their performance for the day. When they are not seeing improvement, they look to what needs to be changed for the next time. Usually, the changes are done in small increments rather than on a massive scale. They seek to constantly improve on each and every performance to get the most out of life.

4) Thrives Under Pressure-Coal into Diamond

Peak performers do not step back from pressure. They welcome and embrace it. Peak performers understand the concept of "coal into a diamond." They know that at the start of their careers, they are not fully formed as peak performance individuals. It will take time and hard work to squeeze the best out of themselves, and they look forward to the challenge.

Pressure and stress are two different things. Peak performers understand that stress is there and not going to go away. In fact, in today's world, there will be new types of stress, such as pandemics and natural disasters. This could impact the world of a peak performer if they let it. Peak performers are always looking for new strategies and tools for managing or eliminating stress. They don't run away from it or look to bury their heads in the sand, hoping it will pass on by.

5) Theatre of The Mind

While we talked about using visualization to see images of success, there is another method that peak performers have been using for approximately 50 years. It was invented by Dr. Maxell Maltz, who was trained as a plastic surgeon. Dr. Maltz discovered that after working on people who were involved in accidents and had suffered facial injuries that his ability to fix the outer damage was not enough. Many reported that they still felt ugly or disfigured even though the surgery had erased all damage.

From this, Dr. Maltz was able to understand that the brain was responsible for "how a person sees themselves." He wrote a groundbreaking book, and the most widely used technique in the book is called "The Theatre of the Mind."

The basic way that a person uses this technique is to sit quietly in a room and bring up a picture of a movie theatre in their mind. They hear the sounds, see the objects and colors, and adjust everything just as a movie director would.

For peak performance, the person is sitting in the audience watching themselves on the big screen, and they begin to perform onscreen, doing their task with peak efficiency. As the performance is elevated with music and the proper lights, the person leaves the audience and walks up to the screen, stepping into the screen and becoming the top performer they knew they always were. Using Theatre of the Mind is not a one-time thing. It is also a skill that must be practiced.

As with regular visualization, some people find it hard to see pictures, colors and hear specific sounds in their minds. Sometimes it takes breaking it into chunks until you learn how to do it. You can work each piece one at a time and, as a real director, edit it, splice it together and make a fantastic movie.

6) Rest and Recharge

Peak performers understand that burnout can be a factor in not achieving success. They schedule rest time to allow their minds and bodies to recharge. Some peak performers will use rest and recharge as reward systems for a job well done. For example, when they hit a milestone, they may head to a weekend spa to totally unwind and clear the mind.

Recently it has been shown that taking two or three days away from electronics such as cellphones and laptops will reset the brain. This will certainly improve peak performance upon returning to the chosen profession. The ability to focus will improve, and decision making will be much easier. Treating the body well pays dividends beyond belief.

To be a peak performer, you need to grow daily. One perfect method is reading something not related to your course work for 30 minutes a day. Feed your mind with the material it needs. Just like plants need sunshine, your brain thrives on knowledge.

Chapter 9:
Your Success Action Plan

*"Lack of direction, not lack of time, is the problem.
We all have twenty-four-hour days." Zig Ziglar*

Where Are You Going In Your Life?

Where are you going in your life? What do you want your life to look like? Why are you still thinking and not doing? It seems that many people struggle to answer the basic question of "what do you want in life?" or "where are you going with your life?" Ask 100 people these questions, and you will get answers that declare what they don't want.

Answers like these:

- I don't want to have a job that sucks when I graduate.

- I don't want to spend any more time in school.

- I don't want to keep driving this same crappy car for another year.

That is a lot of don'ts! It's so much easier to know what we don't want than to clarify what we do want. That is because we innately seem to know that when we declare what we do want - we are committed to it, and we will get it. Are you familiar with the saying, "watch what you pray for; you just might get it!"?

Think about what you have been saying you don't want - isn't that what you have in your life now? Or are you close to experiencing it?

If so, now is the best time to stop and review how your thinking got you where you are now. And now is the best time to change your answers to something that reflects what you do want.

If what you want is a better version of YOU, you're in the right place.

Knowledge + Action = Powerful Results

When we decide that we're ready to change ourselves, we must first understand what needs to be changed. Then we must decide where to begin. Personal development is like putting together a puzzle. When the pieces fit together, the final result is a magnificent, powerful human being. Knowledge is the first piece of the puzzle. We obtain knowledge through class lectures, assignments, tests, books, videos, workshops, and more.

The principles of success that are laid out in this chapter are proven principles for living. They are part of many other principles that have been revealed, written about, taught, and lived by thousands of people over the years. The "fathers" of Success Principles include Napoleon Hill, Wallace Wattles, Orison Swett Marden, and many others.

You've seen them written in books meant to teach you to a specific end: getting rich, improving relationships, changing habits, etc. You now have the knowledge in front of you, ready to be read and learned and implemented – to transform your life.

Action is the second piece of the puzzle. Action means putting into practice what you've read. Practice means doing something every day until you master it. Each success principle includes action steps for you to take. These action steps are designed to show you exactly HOW you begin living the principle. Because it's in the living of the principle that transformation happens.

Putting into action what we've learned is really when transformation happens. You now have the power to transform yourself into a better version of YOU - and that is a wonderful thing.

The Principles Of Success

Action

Action is a principle of success because nothing happens until action is taken. Rally the forces of self-discipline and personal initiative, and you can now take action on your plans. Until you hit a bump in the road!

Whether it's through your course work, club or activities on campus, internships, reading or listening to books, listening to podcasts, or watching videos, you know that success leaves clues. Many people have written about those clues over the last 100 years.

Now it's time for you to achieve your goals. To have wonderful relationships, land the perfect job at graduation, build a thriving business, etc. It's no longer just a thought or dream because you know what you can do each day to make it happen.

What's stopping you? What's holding you back?

If you're like most people, you read the words, watch the videos, and listen to the podcasts. You get inspired and start dreaming about what is possible. You get a glimpse of where you could be in your life. You may even have a clear vision of exactly where you want to be and what you want to be doing with your life.

You're inspired to change your life, to create an amazing story for your life. You get it. You get the importance of success habits. You get the importance of practicing success principles. You understand that happiness and contentment are an inside job. You no longer want to procrastinate! It all makes sense to you. You may even be inspired by the stories you've read of ordinary people, possibly people you've met personally, and thought to yourself, "if they can do it, I can do it!"

So, why are you struggling?

You are struggling because the idea of making these changes, of doing something different each day to change your life, is quite scary. You have found a nice, comfortable, familiar way to live that does not include surprises or changes or dealing with unknowns. After all, it's college. I will deal with all that success stuff when I graduate and get a real job. You feel safe right now. But safe doesn't mean a life of happiness, fulfillment, and financial success.

On a conscious level, you are dealing with tuition, bills that need to be paid, class assignments that need to be done, family and friends who need your attention, and a host of other things that need tending to. And this may not be the Life you say you want, but it's what you have, and you can trust it. You know what to expect. You know how to manage yourself as a student. Changing any of this is what strikes fear into your heart and mind. On the one hand, you can't wait to get finished with school, and you are excited to start your career. The whole adulting thing can be a bit scary and nerve-racking.

Here's the deal: As much as you want to start making success habits a part of your life, as much as you want to experience the freedom that comes from living by the success principles you know work - for others - it's not enough. You must take action now! Do not wait until graduation to start thinking about taking things to the next level. Do it now!

You're not alone. Many have been stuck in that place between knowing and action. The good news is that there is a way to get unstuck. And the way to do it is to start small.

Start Small

Forget trying to talk yourself into changing through sheer willpower or pep talks. That might work for a few days or even a week, but it's not enough.

As important as it is for you to have long-term goals, lifetime achievement goals, 5 year and 10 year goals, it is more important that you're able to put into action the steps necessary to achieve those goals and not get stuck.

Your focus needs to be on doing one small thing at a time. Something you know you can do. And to make it easier to incorporate into your daily life. You can simply stack this new thing right on top or before or after something you're already doing.

When you're able to see progress and feel a difference, you'll be motivated to continue. You'll also be able to see when you are ready to add something else to your daily routine. And you'll know how to do it. Here's how to start small. You're going to commit to doing something different for 30 days.

You can imagine doing something for 30 days. Think of it as a test period. You'll review the results and do it again for the next 30 days. Imagine it's 30 days from now. You've just had the best 30 days of your life. What does that look like?

- Who did you say yes to?

- Who did you say no to?

- Did you make an "A" on your first project?

- Did you add 20 new connections on LinkedIn?

- Did you attend every one of your class lectures?

- Did you finish every assignment 24 hours ahead of the due date?

- Did you lose 5 pounds?

- Did you make your first $1 from your side hustle?

What does it look like, for you, 30 days from today? As you can see by the questions, you can focus on your income, your life, your schoolwork, anywhere you have a goal.

Pick the one thing you want to improve on greatly, and focus your attention on just that one thing. Now, take out your calendar and mark it on your calendar 30 days from today. Next, decide what you are committed to doing differently, every day, for the next 30 days.

How does that fit with your normal daily routine and schedule? Where does it fit? How will you fit it into your day? Before your classes, after lunch, after classes, or dinner? Commit to stopping all busywork. Commit to having more than 50% of your daily activities focused on action steps to achieve your 30-day goal. Commit to adding one thing to your day to help make your dreams a reality.

Attitude

As a success principle, a positive mental attitude means you live in the solution. You prefer to solve problems, learn from challenges. You understand that the current situation is temporary and that you have the power to change it.

Your attitude. It's what determines how you experience the world and, more importantly - how the world experiences you. When you see the world through a positive attitude, you tend to be solution-oriented. This means that when presented with a challenge, a difficulty, a problem, or even a tragedy, you'll ask, "what is the best way through this." You will be more likely to think. Yes, I Can. And, you will have a positive influence on those around you as they begin to see you accepting problems and overcoming challenges.

When you see the world through a negative attitude, you tend to be problem-oriented. This means that when presented with a challenge, a difficulty, a problem, or even a tragedy, you'll ask, "why is this happening to me?" You will more likely to say No, I Can't. And, you will have a negative influence on those around you as they see you as an anchor that stops them from finding a solution and as someone who doesn't handle adversity well at all.

Successful people understand that a positive attitude is what makes things happen in their world.

You say you want to be a more positive person. You want to see problems as challenges. You want to stop blaming others for your problems. You just don't know how to change your thinking.

The change begins when you're willing to see yourself, in action, as a negative person. Make a conscious effort to become aware of when you are negative. Here are some examples that may help you recognize when you have a negative attitude. When you dwell on problems, you say things like:

- "I'm so sick!"

- "I know I'm going to get sick (fall, not wake up on time, etc.)."

- "Why does everyone have to drive like that!?"

- "What an idiot!"

- "You wouldn't catch me doing that."

- "I never get a break!"

- "When is it MY turn?"

- "No way I can do that."

- "How'd they get so lucky?"

- "It won't work for me."

- "See, I screwed up ... again."

Any of these words sound familiar to you? If you say yes, it's time to check yourself. Do you really want to have a positive attitude? Do you really want to have good things happen in your life? Do you really want the peace of mind you see others have? Do you really want the success - that you say you want? If you say yes, there is something you can do to make it happen?

It begins with being willing to practice the principle of a positive mental attitude. Starting now. Likely you just thought to yourself that you will not be able to do it. Or that you don't understand it, so it won't work for you. Stop. Take a deep breath. Say out loud, "Well, isn't that interesting? Let us see how I can change my attitude." When you do this, you are now in solution mode. You are open and willing to hear and learn how this change can happen.

Next is to change from a reactive person into a responsive person. A reactive person waits for something to happen and then reacts with emotion, often without much thought. A responsive person is intentional when responding to an event, thinking it through, understanding the context of the situation, discerning the most effective action for long- and short-term outcomes.

As a student, reactive means not breaking your larger assignments into smaller chunks and working on them throughout the semester. It means cramming for exams the night before the test. It means throwing your assignments together at the last minute. It means skipping one class to do the assignment do in your next class. It means not using a planner and organizing your semester. It means dropping classes and adding a semester or two to your graduation.

In business, being reactive means that strategies have not been given a lot of thought, and often this results in Shiny Object Syndrome - moving from one "fix" to the next with regard to marketing, outsourcing, and management tools.

Here is what it looks like with marketing: You have been dumping money into Facebook ads for a month, you're not making steady sales, and someone in a group says that Instagram ads work better. Then you shift to Instagram ads for a few weeks, and you are not making any sales, so when someone says TikTok is what is working for them, you drop Instagram and move to TikTok.

I think you get the idea. A successful person is a responsive person. They understand that they are in control of their emotions, their thinking, their actions. And, when they are presented with a problem, a challenge, or an opportunity, they take the time to think through the situation so they can act in a way that results in a positive outcome - for themselves and the people around them.

You can become a responsive person by deciding what your attitude will be from this point forward. Just as you did when you decided you would become a person with a positive mental attitude. Commit to thinking before acting.

Become aware of how you react when presented with new situations and stop yourself from saying or doing anything. Take that moment to breathe deeply and think through what is happening. Think through your decision - what will happen if you say no? What will happen if you say yes? Is it possible to wait 24 hours before making the decision? If not, then is it possible to wait an hour? Give yourself time to think through the actions and options and then make your decision based on what you know.

It's right about now when many people will say, "But I'm a Do Whatever It Takes Kind of Person!"

Being resilient and willing to do whatever is necessary to keep your word, finish a project, honor a contract, and stick to your plan is what a successful person does. Anyone who thinks that "do whatever it takes" means to jump in without forethought or planning is setting themselves up to fail.

Action Steps

A. Commit to becoming a person with a positive mental attitude. Say it out loud.

B. Starting now, when you hear yourself saying something negative, stop, breathe, turn it into a solution-oriented statement.

C. Commit to responding and not reacting using the same technique of stop, breath, think through what is happening.

Critical Thinking

Through the ages, Greek philosophers and modern-day personal development experts have discussed the need for every person to develop their critical thinking skills. Today, with the growth of social media and the inability of many people to recognize false news stories and faulty arguments, there is a sense of urgency in these discussions.

As a success principle, critical thinking is aligned most closely with Napoleon Hill's principle of Accurate Thinking. Napoleon Hill refers to our minds as a piece of land that can be used to grow beautiful gardens or can be left alone to be overrun with weeds.

If we want a beautiful garden, we must tend the soil, feed it nutrients, plant seeds that will grow into beautiful flowers and fruits. This takes work based on planning, skills, and tools. Using critical thinking skills takes work. Part of that work involves seeking accurate information by asking questions, comparing answers to determine relevancy to the question, and thorough analysis of the final answers to determine if they are, indeed, the factual and final answers.

What exactly is accurate thinking? How do we know we've received accurate information?

Accurate thinking is based on two types of reasoning:

1. Induction. This is the act of reasoning from the specific to the general, from the individual to the universal. It is based on experience and experimentation, and you can draw conclusions.

2. Deduction. In this act of reasoning, specific conclusions are based on general logical assumptions.

Induction allows for false results. For instance, suppose that every time you throw a rock at a window, the window breaks while the rock remains unchanged. You do this repeatedly, and it causes you to reason inductively that the glass is fragile, and the rock is not. There is a conclusion based on experience that could still be proven inaccurate, but at the moment, it is reasonable.

Deduction starts with a general statement and then examines the possibilities to reach a specific, logical conclusion. For instance, you can take the experience of throwing a rock at a window and reason that another non-fragile object would also break the glass. Or that the rock would also break another fragile object like a china dinner plate. There is a logical connection between the non-fragile object and the fragile object.

So how do you apply this throughout your day? To be an accurate thinker, you must take two important steps:

1. Separate facts from opinions, fiction, unproved hypotheses, and hearsay.

2. Separate facts into two categories: important and unimportant.

One area to apply this process is to other people's opinions. Opinions are everywhere, and almost everyone is willing to share whether they're asked for it or not. And more often than not, these opinions are worthless. These opinions can also be dangerous and destructive, especially when they are shared with great enthusiasm and presented as factual.

The accurate thinker, the critical thinker, will ask for facts to support the opinion expressed. We will want to know what that person is basing the opinion on, and if there are no facts, written or otherwise, ask them to show examples of experience to support those opinions. The critical thinker won't offer an opinion, except when it can be shown to be based on facts.

What you can do is to stop reacting to what other people are saying and begin to question whether the information they share is accurate. The same is true of news stories and reports and especially of gossip and rumor. Without asking for facts, you are relying on unproven information to influence how you make decisions in your life and business. Question ideas and assumptions other people put forth. You want to determine whether the idea, argument, or finding that is stated represents the entire picture or if there is more that needs to be known.

The successful decisions we make in life and business were made because we found no reason to not make them. We can apply the same questioning process when we find ourselves hesitating to make a decision. Ask yourself these questions:

- Will, it hurt someone close to me? Who will be affected, and how?

- Will it benefit me personally? How?

- Will it benefit my company? Will it add to the bottom line or be an expense?

- Does this support my goals for my life? Will it move me forward or backward?

- Does this align with my values? Will I regret my actions if I move forward with this? Why?

The key isn't to just ask questions. It's to ask better questions. Think about the end goal and how the decision you make, the problem you solve, the person you invite into your life affects your ability to achieve that end goal.

Action Steps

A. Write out the questions listed and recall an instance when someone shared an opinion with you. Review that instance with these questions. Can you answer them? If not, it's time to review those questions and commit to asking them the next time someone shares an opinion.

B. Make the decision, now, to ask at least two questions the next time someone shares an opinion or you learn of a news story.

Forgiveness

As a true success principle, forgiveness is what actually frees you from resentments, heals your relationships with family and friends and colleagues, and lets you be at peace with yourself and the events in your life, which means you can experience gratitude and joy more often and at a deeper level.

Forgiveness is something you do for yourself. And by being able to forgive - yourself and others - you can remove the obstacles that are preventing you from reaching your goals.

- Do you think you do not have an issue with forgiveness? Are you sure?

- How do you deal with disappointments?

- How do you deal with criticism?

- How do you deal with rejection, disrespect, betrayal?

The emotional pain caused by others can be the wall that stops you from succeeding. You may think it's a lack of resources, while the reality is that you aren't looking very hard for the resources you need. You may think it's having too much on your calendar and task list, while the reality is that you're living in overwhelm to avoid feeling sad or angry about a situation with someone in your life.

We, humans, are complicated creatures. There is no direct straight line that you can follow from Situation A that leads to Feeling B. Often, we have an initial reaction that we will suppress and think we'll deal with later, only to find ourselves caught up in our daily life challenges.

We think we have moved on from a situation but then find ourselves overreacting to a friend's comment, someone else's anger about a decision we have made, or disruptions while we are working on an assignment. These overreactions are because we did not resolve an experience we had yesterday, last week, last year, many years ago.

How does all this connect to your daily student life? You won't often hear a lot of people talking about forgiveness in a professional context. However, when we can see that other people suffer from emotional pain, for whatever reasons, and to varying degrees, we can see that their actions aren't motivated by something personal to us - they're acting from a feeling of hurt that has nothing to do with us. They're holding on to resentment, feeling the initial anger from a past situation, and thinking it's the current situation they're angry about. Now the question is: are we able to see this in ourselves?

We must learn to deal with people and their negativity, unreasonable requests, surprising overreactions. What if we are doing the same things to other people? What if our communication with others is laced with negativity, snarky comments, and anger? What if we're treating others in a way we don't like to be treated?

We all have attachments to other people; we create bonds based on shared experiences and likes and dislikes. We're not just attracted to like-minded people; we're encouraged by others in our lives to seek the company of like-minded people. It's these attachments that make forgiving ourselves so important.

As we encounter trust issues, grieve the loss of a friendship, wrestle with the feelings of betrayal, we take those feelings into our daily lives, and they affect how we respond to others. While we experience these issues at varying levels, when we don't resolve them right away, we carry them into the next day, the next week, the next year. Then, when we are ready to resolve them, we find ourselves going through the grief process. This is when some people will stop and try to tell themselves that it's just not that important. For those who understand that it is important to resolve these issues, they will get through the grieving process.

Something to remember is that there are eight stages of grief. They are as follows:

1. Denial

2. Anger

3. Sadness

4. Fear about what will happen next

5. Mental and emotional acceptance

6. Forming new attachments or renewing a bond

7. Forgiveness

8. Finding full gratitude and joy again

Of these, forgiveness can be the most difficult. And yet, it's also the most healing. Forgiveness means: to be able to give again. People who are not able to forgive tend to become victims or persecutors. They are unhappy, cynical, negative, over defensive, and they suffer. They tend to hold others hostage by accusing them of actions or thoughts that are causing harm when it's their inability to detach themselves from someone else's emotional issues. The victim and the victim-turned persecutor's attitudes result in one not being able to experience real joy, genuine love, or full gratitude.

Does this sound familiar? Does it describe anyone you know or maybe even describe yourself? If so, there are some things you can do to begin the journey to forgiving yourself. The first thing is to be clear on what it is you want to forgive. Your first thought might be that you know what you've done or didn't do. Are you sure? If time has passed, your perceptions have changed, your recollection can be skewed by today's emotions and knowledge. This is where a journal can help to give you clarity. Write down what happened and your part in it. Stick with the facts.

When you're done, read it and remove the extra parts that have nothing to do with the actual behavior or words that occurred. Be truthful, don't embellish. Next is to acknowledge your emotions around that situation. Give yourself permission to be angry, hurt, frustrated, afraid, sad, embarrassed. Time has passed, but those emotions are still tied to that incident, and if you want to forgive so you can let go, feeling the feelings at this point is essential.

Say or read what you have written out loud. Sometimes, when you give voice to the thoughts in your head and the emotions you're feeling, you hear it differently, and you feel free from the burden. This doesn't always happen, though saying things out loud has proven to reduce the "heaviness" that comes with keeping them suppressed.

And next, think through how you could have handled yourself differently. What would you have done if you had tried to resolve the issue at the time it happened? Get clear about this because it reflects your vision of who you want to be, which may be different than who you are now. It's now when you also acknowledge the other people involved; if the mistake you made hurt another person, you need to determine the best course of action. Do you want to talk to this person and apologize? Are there monetary issues involved? Do you owe them money or cause them to lose money? It may be that to resolve this, you offer to make amends, rather than just an apology. There are steps you take to make amends, some of which include:

- Be truthful about the damage you caused.

- Express your desire to repair it.

- Admit your mistakes.

- Find a way to repair the damage, asking them what they view as fair recompense or repair.

- Be patient if they tell you they don't know yet, and that they'll get back to you.

- Be patient about getting someone's trust; they may not forgive you as readily as you would forgive someone else.

Your intention is to restore goodwill, to make right that which you did wrong, to come clean with your mistakes and missteps so that you don't do them again. It isn't to have the other person say, "I forgive you." The process, when you do it, results in you forgiving yourself.

You will know you have forgiven yourself when you feel a weight lift from your shoulders; you feel a release and feel joyful. Then the feeling turns to be grateful. Grateful for who you are and what you have to offer the world. You will also see the world differently. The grass is greener. The trees are fuller. You will hear birds when before you heard nothing. You will smile when someone cuts you off in traffic. You will find it is easier to communicate with others.

Action Steps

A. Get a pen and paper and write the details of the situation you want to resolve.

B. Once written, read it aloud so that you can hear the details.

C. Determine what action you need to do to resolve the situation so you can forgive yourself.

The Golden Rule

There are two types of forces in this universe. One attracts the other repels. You are a force in and of yourself. You either attract people or repel them. The people you attract are in harmony with your attitude toward life. That is why you attract them. Like attracts like.

Those who have wealth and success in life and business are attracted to each other. Those who have little are attracted to each other.

Which group do you belong to? Do you know?

You may be thinking to yourself that all this sounds a lot like the Law of Attraction. That's because it is very similar. Though the Law of Attraction isn't a success principle. It is a universal law that essentially says, "what you think about, you bring about." Your thoughts are what create your reality, and they are what attract others to you.

In this case, The Golden Rule is a success principle and is based on action. It's your understanding of how your actions are a result of your attitude. It's how you can change your attitude to change your actions.

You may be thinking now that the Golden Rule is "treat others as you would have them treat you." Essentially, that is true. And, if you and others truly believed this and lived it, no one would be getting scammed or cheated or bullied or taken advantage of.

Therein lies the problem. Until everyone is on board with living the Golden Rule, these negative forces will continue to be a part of our lives. The solution is that you decide to practice and live the Golden Rule, share it with others, teach others to live it and be an active part of the solution. Some examples of the actions your attitude can create:

- To expect a full day's pay for doing a half day's work isn't observing the Golden Rule.

- To think only of yourself and your family and forget your duty to your community, your colleagues, your fellow students are not observing the Golden Rule.

- To not pay someone for the service you ordered and they provided is not observing the Golden Rule.

- To expect a grade, you did not earn is not living the Golden Rule.

- To expect an extension on an assignment because you forgot about it is not living the Golden Rule.

Check-in with yourself. Are you thinking and having an attitude like this? If it is, you'll begin to see the reason for your unhappiness and your lack of wealth. You'll also discover your reason for being "unlucky" in life.

The good news is that you can change your attitude. And, by changing your attitude, you can change the attitude of others toward you.

Because, when it comes to achieving success in life and business, it is important that we are able to influence other people to do things that we want them to do. We want them to purchase our products and services. We want them to join our group. We want them to share good things about us with their friends. We want them to collaborate or partner with us.

Some people lie awake nights, knowing exactly how they could make a million dollars, or build a great business, or reduce the cost of living, or offer mankind some other great service if ... they could just get people to do what they wanted them to do! They get caught up in the frustration of not having that power because it never occurs to them that there is a method, a proven, effective method through which we can get other people to do what we want them to do. It begins with you.

Your job is to master yourself and direct your efforts toward the goal you want to achieve, toward becoming the person you want to become. The only way you'll be able to do your job is to ignore those who fail to apply the Golden Rule. Their misfortune is not an excuse for you to ignore it, too.

No one can achieve permanent success unless that success is built on the fundamentals of success principles such as this one.

For the Golden Rule to truly work for you - you must apply it. You must talk about it to others. You must teach others the advantage of applying it. To benefit the most from the Golden Rule, you should work hard to develop a reputation of being a person who believes in and applies the Golden Rule in all human relationships. Yes, that's a lot of work. It's worth the effort. A passive agreement, thinking about it, believing in it is not enough. It is a principle that, when lived and applied in daily life, carries tremendous power to transform you and others.

When you understand the power that is the Golden Rule, you can use it to bring all the happiness and wealth, and material success you want. You can turn enemies into friends, attain greater success in whatever career you have chosen.

Action Steps

    A. What is your attitude, now, about who is to blame for the circumstances in your life?

    B. Are you willing to change your attitude?

    C. Write down what you will commit to doing every day to practice the Golden Rule.

Personal Initiative

As a success principle, personal initiative is vital to your success because it is what fuels your willingness to act. It is your inner power source, and some see it as the internal battery for motivation. It is the enemy of procrastination.

Napoleon Hill has personal initiative as the 9th principle in his book and course, Law of Success. He said, "Success is something you must achieve without someone telling you what to do or why you should do it."

This is really an excellent description of being proactive instead of reactive. Being proactive means you're doing more than what needs to be done, doing the extra work that brings more meaning to life and your course work. There are many successful students, business owners, musicians, artists, athletes, teachers, mothers, fathers, and others who have achieved their goals because they have personal initiative. They didn't have someone telling them what needed to be done. They went and did the work because they understood that it was necessary for them to achieve their goal. Consider this:

- No one told Steve Jobs to continue to create new products. He did it using his own personal initiative.

- No one told Richard Branson to found Virgin Music as a mail-order record business. He did it using his own personal initiative.

- No one told Mary Kay Ash to found Mary Kay Cosmetics. She did it using her own initiative.

- No one told Dolly Parton to seek fame and fortune as a country music writer and singer. She declared her intentions in high school and followed through using personal initiative.

No one pushed these people, and others, to do the things required of them to achieve their goals. It was the consistent use of personal initiative that made it possible for them to accomplish what they did and reach that level of success.

Your goal may be to become a champion athlete, a remarkable actor, a million-dollar salesperson, the owner of a business, a real estate titan. Whatever your goals, if you are going to be successful, you must use personal initiative to do the work, to do the little things, to do what is required of you to succeed.

Beyond achieving your goals, you can expect a few side benefits. These include being respected by your peers and others in your community, being influential in your chosen field, having a solid sense of self and a high level of confidence, and being noticed by other influencers and community leaders.

Andrew Carnegie once said, "There are two types of people who never amount to anything. There are those who never do anything except what they are told to do. And there are those who cannot even do what they are told to do. The people who get ahead do the things that need to be done without being told they have to do them. And they don't stop there. They go the extra mile and do much more than is expected of them."

What does it mean to "go the extra mile?"

It means doing more than the minimum requirement for assignments and ensuring the quality of work is strong, adding a bit more than was agreed upon. I had a student do an interview with an industry expert even though that was not a requirement for the paper. Doing the little extra steps like that demonstrates you cared and took the assignment seriously.

There's a known phrase "a baker's dozen" that is rooted in making sure the total weight of the baked goods was a bit more than expected, so a penalty wasn't incurred. It's become known as the little extra that we often receive from bakeries, produce stalls, and small candy shops. Order 12 and receive 13. Order 24 and receive 25. It's a nice surprise on the part of the customer and invokes a feeling of appreciation for the shop, ensuring that the customer will remember that shop the next time they need that product.

Going the extra mile demonstrates you are willing to do the work, big or small. It demonstrates you are a person of character, someone who can be counted on to deliver. Not everyone has a personal initiative. If they did, we would not have the two types of people Andrew Carnegie refers to. Which type of person do you want to be? The one who never amounts to anything or the one who gets ahead?

Now is the best time to step up your game and distinguish yourself from all the other students in your major. It is also the best time for you to make great progress on your personal goals. You have unique skills and talents and are capable of achieving your goals. If you're stuck, feeling like you're being held back, something to consider is the people you've surrounded yourself with. If they aren't willing to go the extra mile or do the extra work, they could be holding you back. If that's the case, begin adding go-getters and focused, driven people to your circle.

Action Steps

Take a personal assessment of your willingness and commitment to do the work necessary to achieve your goal.

If you find yourself coming up short on that assessment, reach out to those you admire in your field and connect with them so you can be influenced by their personal initiative. What areas of your life or studies can you "add the bit of extra" to? Where can you be of better service?

Planning For Success

Before you can become successful, you must have a definition of what success means to you. In college and in life, we talk about success all the time but rarely do we take the time to define it. If you don't have your own definition, you're not alone. When asked if they want to be successful, most people will respond yes. When asked to describe what success means to them, few can describe it.

Some will stammer a bit or hesitate, then talk about big houses, fancy cars, traveling the world, vacationing at expensive resorts. They talk about the external evidence of the money being spent. And, while these material things are nice, they really aren't evidence of success. They're simply evidence of money being spent.

Others will be silent because they honestly have never given it much thought. Success is a word that is in the title of numerous books and is often said when referring to someone who has achieved great things in life. So, it makes sense that many people associate the ability to purchase material things as a symbol of success.

They're missing out on something very important, though. They're missing out on the deeply satisfying experiences and relationships that come from working toward achieving something great in your life.

By not defining success for themselves and by accepting someone else's definition of success, the result is a lot of unhappy, unfulfilled people in the world. If you're one of those, then now is the best time for you to take time to define what success, for you, really is.

You see, 99% of the population has it backward. They set goals based on what they want to have, fortune, fame, material things. Instead, they should be focused on who they want to become and what things they need to do to become that person. Once you decided that, you should become relentless in your pursuit of becoming that person. When you clearly focus on who you want to become and do the things necessary to become that person, you will have all the things you want.

This approach is not only true in your financial success, but with your relationships as well. Let's say, for instance, you have a vision in your mind for your future spouse or partner. You want somebody smart, good looking, kind, funny, and generous. Ask yourself this question… Am I the type of person that would be attractive to such an individual?   If not, what do I need to do to become the type of person that would attract the kind of person I am looking for?   I call this the Be, Do, Become approach to success.   Get clear on what type of person you want to BE? Determine what things you need to DO to BECOME the type of person you want to BE.   Then become relentless in your pursuit and commitment to making it happen. Follow this approach, and you will HAVE all the things you desire.

Look at the people you admire in life and business. What is it about them that leads you to believe they are successful? Look closely at their relationships with other people, at the respect they have for their peers and colleagues, at their skills and talents that they've been putting to use in their work or business.

You should soon see that what you admire is more than the material things that symbolize the success you believe they have. Now, look at how they got to the point of being successful. This is the path they took to their success and the path that required some planning.

You will need to create a plan for your success, and it begins with defining what success means to you. This is where you decide what success is and how you will know when you achieve it. For many students, they begin with the money, if that's what you believe will show you are successful. Here are a few questions to consider:

- How much money must you have before you think you're successful?

- Is it cash in the bank, or is it tied to investments?

- How will you get that money? Will you use the skills and talents you have now, or will you leverage relationships you have with others?

- Is the money being replenished regularly, or did you somehow get it in one lump sum?

As you can see, there's more to having money as the symbol of success than just - having money.

If you've decided that success means something deeper than just having money, you'll need to look closely at the details involved. If your definition of success is to help people, consider these questions:

- How will you help others?

- Who will you be helping?

- Why do they need or ask for your help?

- What skill or talent will you use to help them?

- How do you know you've succeeded when you've helped them?

Once again, you can see there's more to helping people than just saying you want to. This is how you plan to succeed:

Be clear about what you want to achieve in your life, identify the activities that emotionally satisfy you now, identify what needs to be done along the way to achieve your vision. It sounds simple because it is, though, it isn't easy. The first thing you must address is your willingness to commit to doing the work that needs to be done regularly. Growth in awareness and finances rarely comes in great leaps. It most often comes in small steps.

Think of it this way - if you were handed $1 million right now, would you appreciate the effort it took for someone else to have earned that money? And would you know what to do with it to ensure that it wasn't gone in a year or two?

Planning to succeed gives you time to grow in small steps so that when your success happens, you are ready for it. You are ready to accept it. You are ready to enjoy it. You are ready to be the person you must become to maintain it.

Here is what you can do to create your plan: Take time away from your daily busy work as a student. Away from distractions. Take a couple of days for yourself in a quiet place. Some ideas that might work for you include:

- A weekend in a cabin in the woods or by a lake.

- A couple of days in a hotel or Airbnb in a city a few miles away.

- House sitting for a friend out of town.

- A weekend in a rented RV.

You'll want to bring a pen and notebook with you. You will be doing a lot of thinking and writing notes about what it is you want in life. And, once you have that written down, you will begin to note the action steps necessary to get where you want to be, to become the person you want to be.

The plan isn't intended to be a step by detailed step path to your success. It can't be. Because it's a long-term plan, there will be many obstacles and speed bumps and people that will get in the way or require that you detour for a bit. The point is that you will have a destination clearly defined, and you will know how to recognize it when you arrive.

When you know the final destination, you will find that identifying milestones along the path to that destination isn't difficult. Maybe you need to improve a skill you have. List the people you need to have deeper relationships with that will support your efforts to achieve success.

Determine what other resources you will need and where you can get them. If you don't know where or how don't worry. When you know your destination, the needed resources will become available as you begin working toward that destination.

The Power of a Mastermind Group

Napoleon Hill introduced the world to the concept of a Master Mind and shared it in his book *Think and Grow Rich*: "A mastermind group is designed to help you navigate through challenges using the collective intelligence of others. It is the coordination of knowledge and effort of two or more people, who work toward a definite purpose, in the spirit of harmony."

There are many types of Mastermind Groups. They range from impromptu gatherings of like minds that want to focus on a solution to a problem to regular gatherings of select professionals that discuss all matters of business. There are free groups and paid groups.

There is no better teacher than one who has already done it. And, while they made mistakes and you're likely to make them as well, you can get guidance on how to navigate the path you've selected.

How to Find a Mastermind Group

Determine what you want from the group and if you can give the same in return.

- Is it business guidance and growth?

- Is it personal development?

- Are you planning on entering a specialized industry such as IT, Finance, Insurance? Maybe you want to find a group of professionals in the same industry.

Begin the search for a group:

Ask someone you admire if they are a member of a group. If they are, ask them if you would be able to join. If you aren't eligible, ask for a recommendation to another group. Search online and carefully read the descriptions of the groups you find. Campuses across the country are filled with groups designed to mentor students and foster growth. Whether you find a potential group on campus, off-campus, or online or through a recommendation, contact the leader/owner of the group and ask the following questions:

- How is the group run?

- Is there a limit to the number of members?

- Is there a time limit for each member to discuss an issue/ask a question, or is there a scheduled 'hot seat' opportunity?

- Are there "off-limit" topics?

- Does everyone participate in every meeting?

- What is expected of the group members?

- How are personality clashes or member conflicts resolved?

- Is there a fee?

- How are complaints handled? (if it doesn't meet your expectations)

- Are there testimonials from current or past members you can see?

- What are the membership requirements?

- Is there a formal member agreement?

Action Steps

A. Write why you want to join a mastermind group and what you expect to give and get from being a member.

B. Write the names of people you view as role models.

C. Contact the people on your list and ask if they are a member of a mastermind group or know of one.

D. Search for a mastermind group to fit your needs.

E. Make a note of the type of groups your contacts share with you, what you find online, and the structure/rules/costs for each one.

F. Select a few that you would like to be a part of, contact the owner or moderator of each one, and ask your questions.

G. Join a group

Responsibility

As a success principle, this means you accept full responsibility for the consequences of your actions. Your actions aren't only the physical activity you take to achieve your goal; it is the decisions you make that involve other people as well.

You must take personal responsibility. You cannot change the circumstances, the seasons, or the wind, but you can change yourself. ~ Jim Rohn

There is no such thing as being entitled to a great life. Though it would seem that many think there is. There are heightened levels of expectations about quality career options for college graduates, quality family time, happy personal relationships, and a sense of deep fulfillment in all that we do. And these expectations are based on the fact that we exist. Our mere presence as a human being in the world entitles us to these things.

The reality is quite different. As you, and many others, learn when we begin to participate in society.

The truth is that there is only one person responsible for the quality of the life you live, for the achievement of your goals, for the success you want to experience. That person is you.

If you want to be successful, if you want to achieve your goals, if you want a particular job or house or family or education, you must accept 100% responsibility for everything that you experience in your life. This includes everything: the grades you earn, the decisions you make, the results you produce, the level of physical fitness you have, the level of income you enjoy, all of the debts you incur, every emotion you experience.

That's a lot to be responsible for. It's also a lot to be held accountable for. You are responsible for the level of achievement you reach, and that means you know what needs to be done, you do the work, you maintain the relationships, you stay on track to reach your goal.

This is one of the most difficult things for people to do. And many struggle with it. Because it isn't easy. Most of us have been conditioned to blame others for the parts of our lives we don't like. We never want to see ourselves as the problem.

Successful people don't make excuses for the things that happen to them. They see their experiences as building blocks to becoming the person they want to become. To become a better person. They understand that excuses stop them from achieving their goals. That when they blame someone else, it is taking the attention off of themselves, and that means they can't change anything.

You see, when you believe someone else is responsible for where you are in life, you abdicate control to them. Whereas, when you accept full responsibility for your life, right now, as it is, you have the control. You can change. You can change your thinking, your behavior, your feelings about the people in your life. You now have the freedom to choose the direction, decide the actions, choose the level of productivity you will have in a day, and so much more.

You understand that to be responsible for your actions and for your experience in life means that you're not responsible for the tragedies or disasters, or surprises that happen in life. You are responsible for how you respond to them. Falling into the blame game, making excuses because of something someone else did or didn't do, achieves nothing. Whereas, accepting that the situation has occurred, looking for solutions, and taking action on solutions is achieving something - it is moving you forward toward your goal.

What happens when you make a bad decision that costs you money? The money that you had set aside for rent, a car payment, or tuition? The resulting resentment and anger can be overwhelming if you're not prepared to be accountable for your decision.

What happens when you choose to not resolve a miscommunication between you and a family member? The resulting assumptions on both sides can lead to awkwardness and uneasiness and, eventually, a lack of communication altogether. What happens when you assume someone is attacking you personally when they say they hate your idea? You're unable to hear their feedback and miss out on ideas for improvement.

What happens when you lose a job because the employer doesn't have work for you to do? You see the situation for what it is, feel a little sad that you won't be spending time with your coworkers, and will face some financial struggles, but you roll up your sleeves, and you begin looking for another job. Can you see the difference?

The first step to taking full responsibility for your life is to be willing to be honest with yourself about where you are in life right now.

Take a personal inventory of who you are, how you see other people in your life, the mistakes, and missteps you've made, how you reacted when negative things happened around you. Now commit to responding differently.

There are three key areas you have control over when it comes to responding to the world around you:

1. Your thinking

2. Your behavior

3. Your vision for your life

You get to decide how you will respond when you bomb a test. You get to decide how you will think when someone says something negative about you. You get to decide how you will act when someone behaves inappropriately. You get to decide what you want your life to be tomorrow, next week, next year, in 5 years. You get to decide what you will work on, when you will work on it, how you will work on it, who you will have working with you, and how you will achieve your goals. And, ultimately, you get to decide what kind of person you will be and what you will achieve in life.

Action Steps

A. Identify your excuses.

B. Figure out why you have trained yourself to believe that these things are holding you back from success.

C. Train yourself to have a different view about your excuses and look at each one as a challenge you will overcome.

Self-Discipline

The single most important attribute to becoming successful is self-discipline. Your self-discipline enables you to develop and maintain control and mastery of your thoughts and actions. This means you're able to make better decisions and act on opportunities while ignoring the shiny objects of anything claiming to be new and improved.

It helps you stay focused on doing the things that matter, gives you the motivation to stick with difficult tasks, and gives you the grit to overcome the obstacles and discomfort you experience as you push yourself to accomplish your goals. When we're able to finish what we start, do what we say we're going to do, and accomplish our goals, we increase our confidence, gain the respect of our peers, and are closer to becoming the person we set out to become.

What exactly is self-discipline?

It's the ability to control your impulses, emotions, reactions, and behaviors. With discipline, you're able to say no to short-term or immediate gratification in favor of long-term satisfaction and gain. It's saying "no" when you want to say "yes." And, amazing to some, the more self-discipline you have, the more content you will be with your life. Seriously, you cannot achieve any of your goals without discipline. So, honing this skill is vital to your success.

What it looks like

You don't want to go to the gym, you do it anyway - because you committed to a daily regimen to improve your body. You don't want to finish writing that class paper, you do it anyway. You don't want to attend a fancy dinner event, you do it anyway - because you accepted the invitation and knew the seat at the table is reserved for you. You don't want to pray and meditate, you do it anyway - because you know it will set the tone for the day, and the end results are worth the effort. You don't want to change your thoughts and actions; you do it anyway - because you committed to doing things differently so you could become the person you want to be and achieve the goals you set.

Are you seeing the pattern here? Self-discipline helps you do the things that need to be done so that in the final accounting of your day, month, year, and life, you experience and have all that you wanted.

How to develop self-discipline

It begins with understanding where you are now. What habits are stopping you from achieving your goals and need to be changed or replaced? Procrastination, giving up too soon, eating junk food, always running late, have an excuse for everything are just a few examples of habits that need our attention.

Rather than tackling them all at once, let's pick one and focus on changing it or replacing it so that it no longer stops you from achieving your goals. When you've finished with one, move on to the next. Let's begin with procrastination. There are as many reasons to procrastinate as there are people in the world. For many people, the reason they procrastinate is that they don't have an obvious motivation to do the work. Lack of motivation can be heard as "It's too difficult" or "It's not that important" or "It won't be good enough, so why do it?"

One way to change this thinking, overcome it, replace it is to do it because someone else is involved. There is an old saying that goes, "Don't do it for others; do it for yourself." There are times when you will definitely be more disciplined if you consider how your actions, behaviors, emotions, and impulses affect others. It is okay to use external sources to drive your motivation. Sometimes, those external motivators are more powerful than internal ones.

Next, we can tackle giving up too soon. Stopping before we've reached the finish line. Being discouraged because "it" is taking too long, and you can't see the end in sight. We do this by taking a break and setting aside time to purposefully reconnect with our reason why we decided to do this task or project, how it fits in with our ultimate goal, and what it is supposed to look like when we are finished.

First, remember that you're in this for the long-term gain, not the short-term immediate gratification. Now, revisit your goal. Use your imagination to recall why you set the goal in the first place. What was the reason this task was identified as important in the process for you to achieve your goal? How does it fit, now, to achieving your goal? If you decide it's still important and needs to be done, then use the seven levels deep why process:

1. What is important to you about becoming successful?

2. Why is it important for you to (refer to your answer)

3. Why is it important for you to (refer to your answer)

4. Why is it important for you to (refer to your answer)

5. Why is it important for you to (refer to your answer)

6. Specifically, why is it important for you to _____?

7. Why is it important for you to (refer to your answer)

Here's an example of how this works:

What is important to you about becoming successful? Make more money.

Why is it important for you to make more money? Get out of debt.

Why is it important for you to get out of debt? To stop working so hard for other people.

Why is it important for you to stop working? I want to do things with my life with the fruits of my labor.

Why is it important for you to do things with your life with the fruits of your labor? To take care of my family that sacrificed so I can get my college degree.

Specifically, why is it important for you to take care of your family? My family has sacrificed for me, and now it's my turn.

Why is it important for you to take care of your family? Because I want to be the one who helps my family the right way. It's important that they are cared for and looked after by someone who cares rather than depending on the kindness of others.

You should see, by now, that this exercise can help you to get in touch with the reason why you started this college adventure and can reignite the motivation you need to keep doing the work to achieve your goal.

If you want your life to look and feel and be a certain way, you must develop the discipline to get from where you are now to where you want to be. It may seem counterintuitive, but you will find yourself happier and healthier the more self-disciplined you become.

Action Steps

A. Write down the habits that are stopping you from succeeding.

B. Select one to change or replace.

C. Determine how it can be changed or replaced.

D. Commit to doing the new action every day for the next 30 days.

Conclusion

As you have now learned, procrastination is a much more complex issue than most people realize. On our journey together, we have identified what procrastination really is. We have discovered why people procrastinate, and how to identify the root causes of our procrastination, and of course, how to overcome procrastination.

We reach our full potential and the level of success we desire when we stop procrastinating and have a clear understanding of where we want to go. We do not just gain knowledge; we put what we learn into action. You now have new information and guidance on how to get clear on your goals, your big why, and you know the success principles that will help make your dreams a reality.

Success principles in action require us to practice these principles daily. The goal is to master them and to have them become a way of thinking and living, so you do not have to think about applying them. You simply apply them. It takes time to master new ways of thinking and behaving, so be patient with yourself.

Focus on just today and what you can do differently today. Track what you are doing and what you are learning about yourself each day. It is the small things you do each day that add up to big changes. By changing your mindset, getting clear on your path forward, you will find that your struggles with procrastination disappear.

About The Author

Dennis Stemmle is the creative and driving force behind College Success Academy as its founder and Chief Evangelist. As a business leader and educator with over two decades of experience, Dennis brings a unique perspective that bridges the divide between the classroom and the "so-called" real world.

Dennis simply distills the best of the best information and strategies available for college success, mixing his street-tested principles with those of teachers and students from around the country. He is also a best-selling author, successful entrepreneur, speaker, and Lecturer in the Department of Management and Decision Science at Coastal Carolina University.

Follow Dennis on Instagram and Twitter @DennisStemmle and on Facebook @CollegeSuccessAcademy.

Visit Dennis online at CollegeSuccessAcademy.com and learn more ways you can be successful in college.

Made in the USA
Monee, IL
13 April 2021